HBJ
LANGUAGE

1

Dorothy S. Strickland
Richard F. Abrahamson
Roger C. Farr
Nancy R. McGee
Nancy L. Roser

1

Karen S. Kutiper
Patricia Smith

HBJ
LANGUAGE

HBJ **HARCOURT BRACE JOVANOVICH, PUBLISHERS**
Orlando   San Diego   Chicago   Dallas

Acknowledgments

For permission to reprint copyrighted material, grateful acknowledgment is made to the following sources:

Crown Publishers, Inc.: From *Down by the Bay,* a Raffi Songs to Read™ Book. Copyright © 1987 by Troubadour Learning, a division of Troubadour Records Ltd. Abridged text and illustrations from *Imogene's Antlers* by David Small. Copyright © 1985 by David Small.
E. P. Dutton, a division of NAL Penguin Inc.: "If" from *Me* by Inez Hogan. Copyright 1954 by Inez Hogan, renewed 1982 by Frank Hogan.
Greenwillow Books, a division of William Morrow and Company, Inc.: Text and illustrations from pp. 1–2, 20–24, and 27–30 in *Higher on the Door* by James Stevenson. Copyright © 1987 by James Stevenson.
Harper & Row, Publishers, Inc.: "Giraffes Don't Huff" from *Roar and More* by Karla Kuskin. Copyright © 1956 by Karla Kuskin. "Things That Sing" from *All That Sunlight* by Charlotte Zolotow. Text copyright © 1967 by Charlotte Zolotow.
Spike Milligan Productions Ltd.: "My Sister Laura" from *Silly Verse for Kids* by Spike Milligan.
Marian Reiner: From "The Little Hill" by Harry Behn in *Crickets and Bullfrogs and Whispers of Thunder* by Harry Behn, poems selected by Lee Bennett Hopkins. Copyright 1949, 1953, © 1956, 1957, 1966, 1968 by Harry Behn; copyright © renewed 1977 by Alice L. Behn.
Marian Reiner, on behalf of Myra Cohn Livingston: "Wide Awake" from *Wide Awake and Other Poems* by Myra Cohn Livingston. Copyright © 1959 by Myra Cohn Livingston.
Marian Reiner, on behalf of Eve Merriam: From "Me Myself and I" in *There Is No Rhyme for Silver* by Eve Merriam. Copyright © 1962 by Eve Merriam. All rights reserved.
Scholastic Inc.: From *A Book About Pandas* by Ruth Belov Gross. Copyright © 1980, 1982 by Ruth Belov Gross.
United Educators, Inc.: "The Harbor" by Olive Beaupré Miller from *In the Nursery of My Book House,* edited by Olive Beaupré Miller. © by United Educators, Inc.

Art Acknowledgments

Cheryl Arnemann: 17–20; Alex Bloch: 250, 254; Tom Bobrowski: 54–55; Deborah Borgo: 12–16, 122; Olivia Cole: 249, 252; Rick Cooley: 69, 281, P7; Wendy Crockett: 32, 221, 237; Robin Cuddy: 94–95, 231; Don Dyen: 7, 9, 10, 90–91, 174, 187, 196; Len Ebert: 64, 128–129, 156; Marlene Ekman: 8; Simon Galkin: 224, 227–228, 248, 251; Ron Grauer: 78, 103; Lane Gregory: 2, 33–36, 102, 123, 139, 209–210, 236; Dana Gustafson: 70, 140, 142, 212, 214, 244; Llyn Hunter: 56–57, 66, 92–93, 113, 134–135, 160–161, 204–205, 232–233; Susan Jaekel: 67, 89, 158–159; Loretta Lustig: 175, 193, 255–256, P13, P15; Laurie Marks: 68, 168–169, 206–207; Fred Marvin,

52–53; Jane McCreary: 11, 60–61, 96, 100, 104, 112, 115, 126–127, 162–163, 172, 198–199, 208, 234–235; Masami Miyamoto: 253, P11; Christine McNamara: 98–99, 173; Carol Nicklaus: 157; Rik Olson: 83–84, 86, 88, 110, 117–118, 121, 149, 151–154, 170–171, 184, 225–226; Sharron O'Neil: 42–43, 58–59, 130–131, 166–167, 192, 202, 240; Stella Ormai: 22–31, P5; Cindy Salans Rosenheim: 101, 132–133, 216, 220; Mira Shallcross: 80–82, 108–111, 114, 116, 119–120, 155, 190, 222–223; DJ Simison: 124–125, 137, 230, 241, P17, P21; Rosiland Solomon: 3–6, 41, 45–46, 47, 50–51, 200–201, 210, 242–243, P23, P25; Susan Spellman: 136, 194, 211; Dorothy Stott: 144–147; Robert Taylor: 188–189; Barbara Todd: 105, 140, 213; Tom Vroman: 116, 152, 188, 224.

Cover: Tom Vroman

Production and Layout: The Hampton-Brown Company

Photo Acknowledgments

READINESS: 1, Lee Hocker; 21, Tom G. O'Neal/TGO Photography.
UNIT 1: 37, HBJ Photo/Jerry White; 38 (l), Tom G. O'Neal/TGO Photography; (r), Tom G. O'Neal/TGO Photography; 39 (l), Tom G. O'Neal/TGO Photography; (r), Tom G. O'Neal/TGO Photography; 40 (t), Tom G. O'Neal/TGO Photography; (b), Tom G. O'Neal/TGO Photography; 41, Tom G. O'Neal/TGO Photography; 42, Tom G. O'Neal/TGO Photography; 44, HBJ Photo/Jerry White; 45, HBJ Photo/Jerry White; 48 (t), HBJ Photo/Jerry White; (b), HBJ Photo/Jerry White; 49, HBJ Photo/Jerry White; 62, Elliot Smith.
UNIT 2: 73, Tom G. O'Neal/TGO Photography; 79, Karen Rantzman; 80, Tom G. O'Neal/TGO Photography; 81, Tom G. O'Neal/TGO Photography; 85 (l), Tom G. O'Neal/TGO Photography; (r), Tom G. O'Neal/TGO Photography; 87, Tom G. O'Neal/TGO Photography.
UNIT 3: 107, HBJ Photo/Rob Downey; 108, Lee Hocker; 109, Lee Hocker; 110, Lee Hocker; 112, Lee Hocker; 114, Elliot Smith; 115, Elliot Smith; 116, Elliot Smith; 119, Elliot Smith; 121, Elliot Smith; 138 (t), Elliot Smith; (b), Elliot Smith.
UNIT 4: 143, HBJ Photo/Jerry White; 148, Lee Hocker; 149, HBJ Photo/Jerry White; 152, HBJ Photo/Jerry White; 154, HBJ Photo/Jerry White; 164 (l), Karen Rantzman; (c), Karen Rantzman; (r), Karen Rantzman; (b), Karen Rantzman; 165 (l), Karen Rantzman; (c1), Karen Rantzman; (c2), Karen Rantzman; (r), Karen Rantzman.
UNIT 5: 179, Tom G. O'Neal/TGO Photography; 180, The Image Bank; 181 (l), Kjell B. Sandved/S.I. Washington D.C.; (r), Bruce Coleman Inc.; 182, Photo Researchers; 183,

continued at the back of the book

Contents

Telling About Your Class

Reading ↔ Writing Connection

Composition Focus: Class Experience Story

Language Focus: Sentences

Telling About Yourself

Sharing Your News

Building Rhymes

Reading ↔ Writing Connection

Composition Focus: Poem

Language Focus: Action Words

5 Telling What Things Are Like

Reading ←→ Writing Connection

Composition Focus: Description

Language Focus: Describing Words

6 Telling Stories

Reading ◄► Writing Connection

Composition Focus: Story

Language Focus: Capital Letters and End Marks

Dear Student,

Have you ever listened to a story? Have you ever told anyone the way you feel? Have you ever laughed at a joke? Have you ever made a birthday card for someone? Then you have used your language, English.

This book is called HBJ Language. It will help you learn more about English. We hope you have fun learning about your language.

Sincerely,
The Editors

Composition Readiness

Teacher: Children discuss the photograph.

1 Listening to a Poem

Listen to the poem.
What does the poem tell about?

Me Myself and I
by Eve Merriam

Isn't it strange
That however I change,
I still keep on being me?

Though my clothes get worn out,
Though my toys are outgrown,
I never grow out of me.

Teacher: Read aloud the poem and discuss it with children.

2 **Making a Book About Me**

Draw a picture of yourself.
Write about the picture.

Here is a picture of me.

Name _____

Draw a picture of your family.
Write about the picture.

Here is my family.

_____
- - - - - - - - - - - - - - - - - - - -
_____
_____
- - - - - - - - - - - - - - - - - - - -
_____

Name _____

Draw a picture of your friends.
Write about the picture.

These are my friends.

Teacher: Children draw pictures and write or dictate sentences.   COMPOSITION READINESS   **5**

Name _____

Draw a picture of something you like to do.
Write about the picture.

This is something I like to do.

_____
- - - - - - - - - - - - - - -
_____
- - - - - - - - - - - - - - -
_____

Teacher: Children draw pictures and write or dictate sentences.

3 Talking to Others

Talk about the picture.
Who is listening?
Who is talking?

Teacher: Children identify and discuss listening and speaking skills.   COMPOSITION READINESS   **7**

Name _____

4 Listening for Details

Listen and follow directions.

Teacher: See the *Teacher's Edition* for complete directions.

Name _____

 Following Directions

Listen and follow directions.

▲

_____

★

✿

■

Teacher: See the *Teacher's Edition* for complete directions. COMPOSITION READINESS **9**

Name _____

6 Giving Directions

How do you make a mask?
Trace the words and tell what happens
<u>first</u>, <u>next</u>, and <u>last</u>.

first

next

last

Teacher: See the *Teacher's Edition* for complete directions.

Name _____

7 Talking with Actions

Listen and follow directions.

Name _____

8 Listening to a Story

Listen to the story.
What happens first, next, and last?

The City Mouse and the Country Mouse

Teacher: Read aloud the story in the *Teacher's Edition.*

Name _____

9 Listening for Order

Listen and follow directions.
Write the numbers <u>1</u>, <u>2</u>, and <u>3</u>.

Teacher: Children use the pictures to retell the story in order.

Name _____

10 Finding Left and Right

Listen and follow directions.

left   **right**

1.

2.

HBJ material copyrighted under notice appearing earlier in this work.

3.

 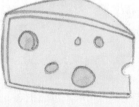

Name _____

11 Using the Telephone

Talk about the picture.
Write your telephone number.

My telephone number is

_____

- - - - - - - - - - - - - -

_____

Teacher: Children discuss how to use a telephone.

Name _____

 Telling a Story

Teacher: Children use pictures to tell, write, or dictate a story.

COMPOSITION READINESS **17**

Name _____

Telling a Story

_____
- - - - - - - - - - - - - - - - - - - -
_____
- - - - - - - - - - - - - - - - - - - -
_____
- - - - - - - - - - - - - - - - - - - -
_____
- - - - - - - - - - - - - - - - - - - -
_____

Name _____

Telling a Story

Name _____

Telling a Story

Language Readiness

Teacher: Children discuss the photograph.

Name _____

 Listening to a Story

Listen to the story.
Then tell what each character does.

Jack and the Beanstalk

Teacher: Read aloud the story in the *Teacher's Edition.*

Name _____

Name _____

Name _____

2 Using Sentences

Talk about the pictures.

Teacher: Children write sentences
about the pictures.

Name _____

 3 Identifying Naming Parts of Sentences

Listen and follow directions.

giant

wife

Jack

Teacher: See the *Teacher's Edition* for complete directions.

4 Identifying Telling Parts of Sentences

Listen and follow directions.

1.

counts

eats

2.

climbs

chops

3.

cries

smiles

HBJ material copyrighted under notice appearing earlier in this work.

Name _____

5 **Matching Sentence Parts**

Listen and follow directions.

1.

Jack

sleeps.

2.

Giant

grow.

3.

Mother

runs.

4.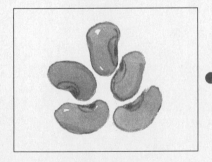

Beans

throws.

Teacher: See the *Teacher's Edition* for complete directions.

Name _____

6 **Completing Telling Sentences**

Finish the sentences.
Use the words in the picture.

1. Jack holds the ____COW____.

2. _____ buys fruit.

3. She pays with _____.

Teacher: Children use the labels in the
picture to complete the sentences.

LANGUAGE READINESS **29**

Name _____

7 Finishing Asking Sentences

Finish the asking sentences.
Use the words in the picture.

Jack

giant

gold

1. Who took my ___  gold ___?

_____

2. Where is the _____?

_____

3. Are you _____?

Teacher: Children use the labels in the picture
to finish the sentences.

HBJ material copyrighted under notice appearing earlier in this work.

Name _____

⑧ Writing ABC Order

a b c d e f g h i j k l m
n o p q r s t u v w x y z

Write the missing letters.

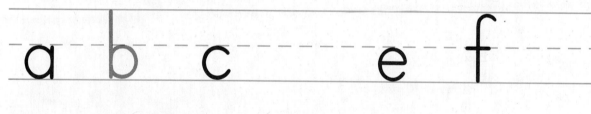

a b c _ e f

h i _ k _ m

o _ q _ s t

w x y _

Name _____

Practicing ABC Order

a b c d e f g h i j k l m
n o p q r s t u v w x y z

Connect the letters in ABC order.
Color the picture.

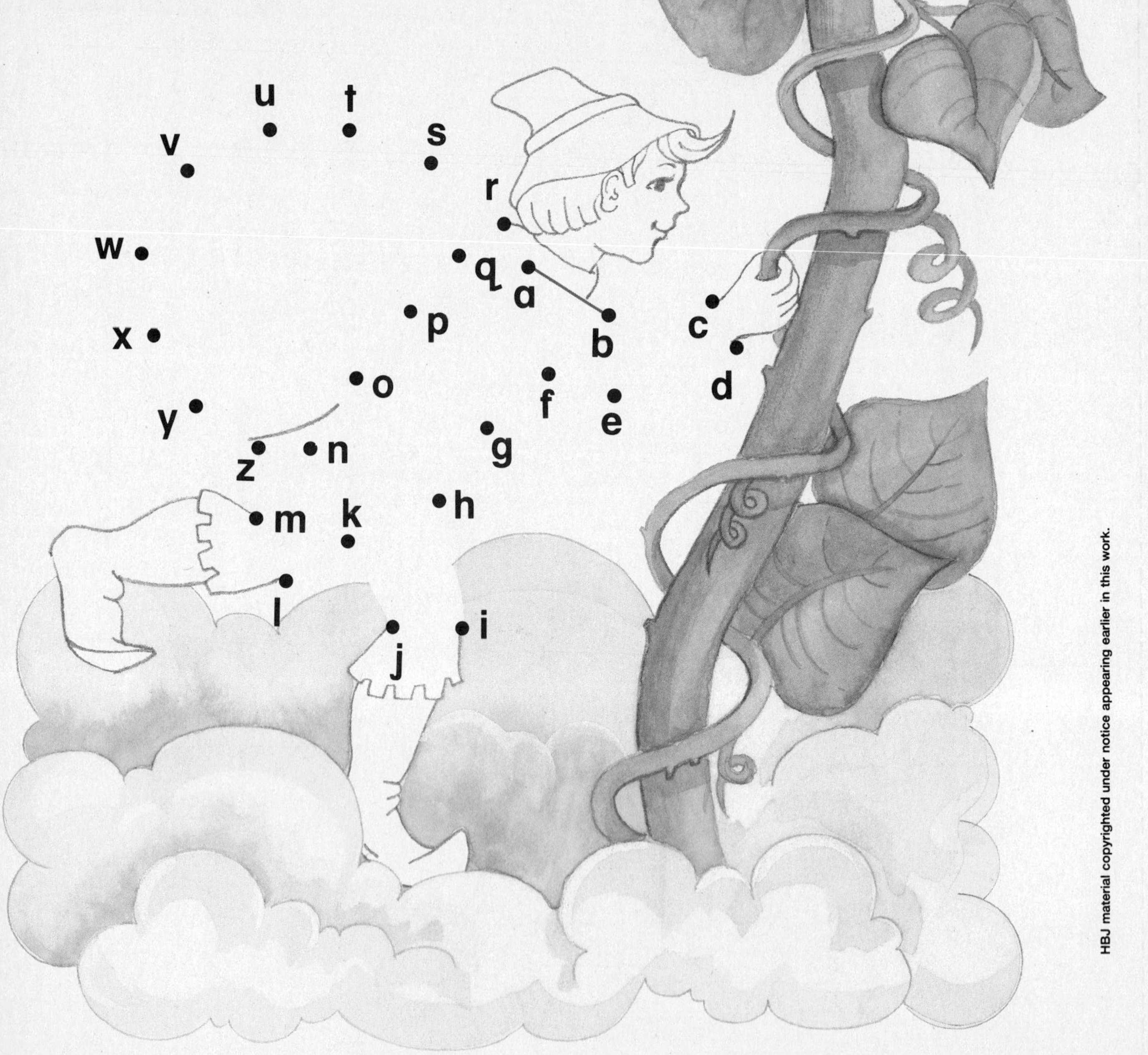

u t
v s
r
w q a
p b c
x f
y o e d
z n g
m k h
l i
j

Teacher: Children connect the letters in ABC order.

Name _____

 Telling a Story

Tell a story about the pictures.
Make a storybook.

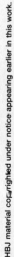

Teacher: Children use the story pictures to
tell, write, or dictate a story.

Name _____

Telling a Story

Telling a Story

Name _____

Telling a Story

UNIT

1

Telling About Your Class

◆ **COMPOSITION FOCUS:**
Class Experience Story
◆ **LANGUAGE FOCUS: Sentences**

Teacher: Children discuss the photograph.

Name _____

Reading with a Writer's Eye

Listen to the story.
Tell the story.

Furry Boy
by Marion W. Crume

_____

- -

_____

- -

_____

- -

_____

Teacher: Read aloud the story in the *Teacher's Edition.* Children dictate or write sentences to retell it.

Thinking As a Writer
Studying a Class Experience Story

Sally and Tommy's class wrote this story.
Listen to the story.
What is the story about?
What happens in the story?

Our Class Pet

Our class pet is a rabbit. His name is Furry Boy. We clean his cage and give him food. We fill his bowl with water. He likes to eat lettuce. Sometimes we feed him cabbage leaves.

Teacher: Read and discuss the class story with children.

Thinking As a Writer
Choosing Details for a Topic

Sally and Tommy's class wrote a story about Furry Boy.
What did the class tell about their pet?
Draw a line from Furry Boy to the things they wrote about.

Teacher: Children connect the pictures about the story.

Listening and Speaking
Listening to Find the Topic

Listen to the story.
Draw a line around the picture that tells what the story is about.

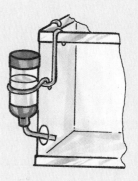

Teacher: Read aloud the story in the *Teacher's Edition.*
Children identify the story topic.

Choosing a Story Idea

Mr. Keller's class wanted to write a story to share with visitors.
First, they talked about things they had done.
Then, they chose to write about their garden.

Try Your Hand

Talk about things your class has done.
Choose one idea for a story.

WRITING PROCESS

Teacher: Children discuss and choose a story topic.

Making a List

The class talked about their garden.
They made a list.
Everything on their list told about
their garden.

Our Garden

planted seeds
watered them
grew tomatoes and beans
tasted good

Try Your Hand

Think about what you would like to tell.
Talk about your story idea.
Help your class make a list of things to write.

WRITING PROCESS

Teacher: Children generate details for a story topic.   COMPOSITION: PREWRITING   **45**

2 | Writing a Class Experience Story

The children read the list.
They thought of things to write about the garden.
They told their teacher what to write.

Our Garden

We planted a garden.
First we planted some
seeds. Then we watered
them. Soon we had
beans and tomatoes.
We ate some. They
tasted good.

Try Your Hand

Read your list.
What would you like to tell?
Help write a story your
class can share.

Who? Why?
What?

WRITING PROCESS

Teacher: Children use their ideas to dictate a story.

3 Adding to Your Story

The class talked about their story.
They wanted to add something.
Talk about what they added.

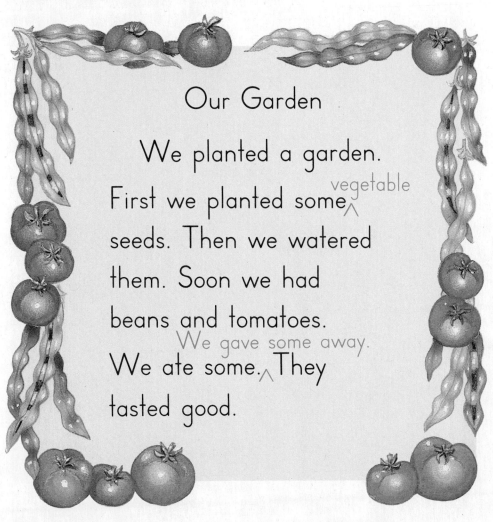

Our Garden

We planted a garden.
First we planted some vegetable
seeds. Then we watered
them. Soon we had
beans and tomatoes.
We gave some away.
We ate some. They
tasted good.

Try Your Hand

Talk about your class story.
What would you like to add?

Use this mark ∧ to add.

We plant flower seeds.
We plant flower seeds.

WRITING PROCESS

Teacher: Children discuss their story
and add to it.

COMPOSITION: RESPONDING/REVISING **47**

4 Sharing Your Story

The children talked about ways
to share their story.
Look at what they did.

First, Mr. Keller made a clean copy of their story.

Then, the class made drawings to go with the story.

WRITING PROCESS

Teacher: Children discuss the pictures.

Last, the class added their story to a bulletin board.

Our Garden
We planted a garden. First we planted some vegetable seeds. Then we watered them. Soon we had beans and tomatoes. We ate some. We gave some away. They tasted good.

Try Your Hand

How could you share your class experience story? Choose one way to share it.

WRITING PROCESS

Teacher: Children publish their class story.

Name _____

Writing in the Content Areas
Science

What kind of pet would you like to have?
How would you take care of it?
Draw a picture of your pet.
Write a sentence.
Tell how you would take care of it.

Teacher: Children write or dictate sentences about their pictures.

CONNECTING
WRITING AND LANGUAGE

Your class wrote a story about one idea.
Each thing you told was written in a separate sentence.
Sentences help build a story.
Read this class story.

Our Turtle

Our class has a turtle.

His name is Tom.

Tom has a hard shell.

Tom eats bugs.

Each box has one sentence.
Each sentence tells something about the story idea.
You will learn about sentences on the next pages.

Name _____

1 Sentences

◆ A **sentence** tells a complete idea.

A sentence is a group of words.
It tells a complete idea.
A sentence begins with a capital letter.

The children talk.

▶ Draw a line around each sentence.

1. The swing is fun.   **2.** is my friend

3. wants to play   **4.** Here is Ann.

Write the sentences.

5. The swing is fun.

6. _____

    Teacher: Children identify and write sentences.

Name _____

THINK AND REMEMBER
◆ Use a **sentence** to tell a complete idea.

Practice

■ Write each sentence correctly.

ann wants to play.

7. Ann wants to play.

she finds the girls.

8. _____

they play jump rope.

9. _____

we turn the rope.

10. _____

ema jumps high.

11. _____

2 Naming Parts of Sentences

◆ A sentence has a **naming part.**

My father reads a story.

Every sentence has a naming part.
The naming part tells <u>who</u> or <u>what</u> the sentence is about.

1. This book is funny.

2. The children like it.

▶ Write the naming part of each sentence.

1. My sister listens.

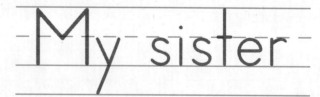

2. A toy is in her arms.

3. Meg looks at the book.

Teacher: Children identify and write naming parts of sentences.

Name _____

THINK AND REMEMBER

◆ Use a **naming part** to tell <u>who</u> or <u>what</u> a sentence is about.

Practice

■ Finish each sentence.

You may use words from the box.

Who		What	
Dad		One picture	
His son		The book	

4. ___Dad___ reads aloud.

5. _____ laughs.

6. _____ has pictures.

7. _____ shows a tree.

3 **Telling Parts of Sentences**

◆ A sentence has a **telling part.**

Every sentence has a telling part.
The telling part tells what someone or something does.

    1. John eats breakfast.

    2. Mother sees the bus.

▶ Draw a line around the telling part in each sentence.

    1. The bus passes our house.

    2. John runs out.

    3. He waves at the bus.

Teacher: Children identify and write telling parts of sentences.

Name _____

THINK AND REMEMBER
◆ In a sentence, use a **telling part** to tell what someone or something does.

Practice
■ Draw a line from each naming part to its telling part.
Write each sentence.

4. The bus •   • opens.

5. Its door •   • stops.

6. John •   • smile.

7. His friends •   • gets on.

8.  The bus stops.

9. _____

10. _____

11. _____

Name _____

◆ Words in a sentence are in order.

Words in a sentence must be in order to make sense.

The girls hold the kittens.

▶ Draw a line under the sentences that are
in the correct order.

1. The kittens need a home.

2. jumps A out. kitten

3. One boy sees the kittens.

Teacher: Children identify and write
sentences using correct word order.

Name _____

Practice

■ Write each sentence in order.

Kim sign. the fixes

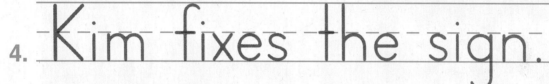

4. Kim fixes the sign.

kitten. Bob holds a

5. _____

purrs. kitten That

6. _____

happy. The is boy

7. _____

home. A kitten a has

8. _____

Name _____

◆ A **telling sentence** tells about something or someone.

A telling sentence begins with a capital letter.
It ends with a period (**.**).

The soup is good**.**

▶ Draw a line around each telling sentence that is correct.

1. My family sits down.   my family sits down

2. we eat   We eat.

3. I like soup.   i like soup

Teacher: Children identify and write telling sentences.

Name _____

THINK AND REMEMBER

◆ Begin a **telling sentence** with a capital letter.

◆ End a **telling sentence** with a period (**.**).

Practice

■ Write each telling sentence correctly.

my family is hungry

4. My family is hungry.

mom asks for lunch

5. _____

a man brings food

6. _____

my brother has soup

7. _____

we like our food

8. _____

6 Asking Sentences

◆ An **asking sentence** asks about something or someone.

An asking sentence begins with a capital letter.
It ends with a question mark (**?**).

I s this your dog **?**

▶ Draw a line under each asking sentence.

1. What is your dog's name?

2. His name is Doc.

3. Where do you live?

Teacher: Children identify and write asking sentences.

THINK AND REMEMBER

◆ Begin an **asking sentence** with a capital letter.

◆ End an **asking sentence** with a question mark (**?**).

Practice

■ Write each asking sentence correctly.

how old is Doc

4. $\underline{\text{How old is Doc?}}$

who feeds him

5. _____

what does he eat

6. _____

does Doc play

7. _____

Name _____

7 Sentences That Show Strong Feeling

◆ Some sentences show strong feeling.

A sentence that shows strong feeling
begins with a capital letter.
It ends with a special end mark (**!**).

T his is fun !

▶ Draw a line around each sentence
that shows strong feeling.

1. We can win!

2. She has the ball.

3. There they go!

Write the sentences that show strong feeling.

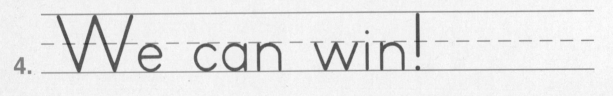

4.

5.

HBJ material copyrighted under notice appearing earlier in this work.

Teacher: Children identify and write sentences
that show strong feeling.

Name _____

THINK AND REMEMBER

◆ Begin a sentence that shows strong feeling with a capital letter.

◆ End a sentence that shows strong feeling with a special end mark (**!**).

Practice

■ Finish these sentences that show strong feeling.
Use words from the box.

You
The game
We
Our team

_____ can do it!

6. $\underline{You \ can \ do \ it!}$

_____ are winning!

7. _____

_____ has the ball!

8. _____

_____ is over!

9. _____

Building Vocabulary
Question Words

Look at the picture.
Read the asking sentences.
Each asking sentence begins
with a question word.

What?	When?
Where?	Who?

When is the party?
Where do
you live?

Practice

■ Finish each asking sentence.
Write a question word.

1.  Who _____ talks on the telephone?

2. _____ does she talk about?

3. _____ does the party begin?

4. _____ is your house?

Teacher: Children write question words.

Name _____

Listening and Speaking

Poetry

Listen to this poem.
Then read aloud the poem with your class.

If
by Inez Hogan

What would you say
If you saw a bear
Sitting on a kitchen chair?

What would you think
If you heard a roar
And saw a lion
Walk in the door?

What would you be
If you could be
A bear, a lion,
Or a chimpanzee?

What would you do
If you could do
Anything you wanted to?

(vertical side text) HBJ material copyrighted under notice appearing earlier in this work.

Teacher: Read aloud the poem. Children
participate in a choral reading.

LISTENING AND SPEAKING **67**

Language Enrichment
Sentences

Learn a Cheer

1. Sit in a circle with your classmates.

2. Have one classmate ask you these questions.

Who are you?
What do you do?

3. Answer the questions.

My name is <u>Michael</u>.
I ride my bike.

4. Have another classmate say this sentence with your name.

<u>Michael</u>, <u>Michael</u>
joins the rest

First-grade children
are the best!

5. Ask everyone to say this sentence that shows strong feeling.

Teacher: Children learn and recite a class cheer.

Name _____

CONNECTING
LANGUAGE AND WRITING

park

Sue

Juan

ball

Tell about the picture.
Write a telling sentence.
Write an asking sentence.
Write a sentence that shows strong feeling.

1 Unit Checkup

Class Experience Story   pages 41–42

Beth's class wrote a book. Here is one story from the book.
Read the story and follow the directions.

> ### Our Visit to the Library
>
> Our class went to the library.
> Mrs. Storm was there. She showed
> us some books. Then she read
> to us.

1. Draw a line under the answer to the question.
   What did Mrs. Storm do?

   a. She read to the class.   **b.** She sang to the class.

2. Draw a line under the picture that shows
   what the class wrote.

   Teacher: Read aloud the directions for each exercise.

Writing Process   pages 44–49

Beth's class wanted to add to their story.
Draw a line around the part they added.

3.

> Mrs. Storm was there. She showed
> us some books. Then she read
> to us.   We thanked her.
>   ∧

Sentences   pages 52-53

Draw a line around each sentence.

4. Matt plays a game.   **5.** is fun

6. are his friends   **7.** We play with him.

Naming and Telling Parts of Sentences   pages 54-57

Finish each sentence.
Use the words in the box.

| sits | Kim | The dog |

8. _____ calls her dog.

9. Muffin _____ .

10. _____ gets a bone.

Word Order in Sentences   pages 58–59

Find the sentences that are in the correct order.
Draw a line under them.

11. make a card I for Dad.

12. His birthday is today.

13. We have a party.

Telling and Asking Sentences   pages 60–63

Draw a line under each telling sentence.

14. We go to the store.   **15.** Do you want milk?

16. Mom buys apples.   **17.** I like red apples.

Now write the asking sentence.

_____

18. _____

Sentences That Show Strong Feeling   pages 64–65

Draw a line under each sentence that shows
strong feeling.

19. Do you see the man run?

20. Look at him go!

21. He runs fast!

2

Telling About Yourself

◆ **COMPOSITION FOCUS:** Story About You
◆ **LANGUAGE FOCUS:** Naming Words

Teacher: Children discuss the photograph.

Reading with a Writer's Eye

Listen to the story.
Tell the story.

from **Higher on the Door**
by James Stevenson

_____

- -

_____

- -

_____

- -

_____

Teacher: Read aloud the story in the *Teacher's Edition.*
Children dictate or write sentences to retell it.

Name _____

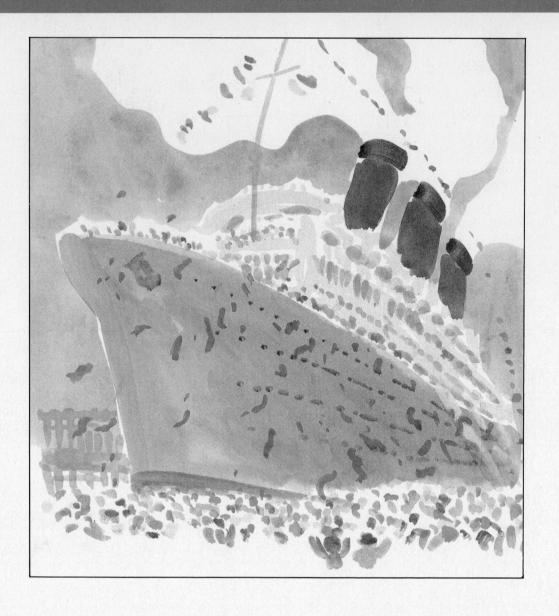

_____

- -

_____

_____

_____

- -

_____

Thinking As a Writer
Studying a Personal Story

Listen to part of <u>Higher on the Door</u>.
Talk about what the writer wrote.
What does he tell about himself?

I have a grandson now. That's how old I am.
But sometimes I look back and remember.
Sometimes our family would take the train
to New York City. When the train for New York
arrived, we'd climb aboard. My father was used to
going on the train, so he read the newspaper.

Teacher: Children discuss what the paragraphs tell about the writer.

Thinking As a Writer
Telling a Story in Order

James Stevenson wrote about a train ride.
What happens first, next, and last?
Draw lines to show what James does.

First •

Next •

Last •

Teacher: Children draw lines to recall story order.

Listening and Speaking
Telling a Story

What is happening in this picture?
What do you think the girl is saying?

Think about a story you would like to tell.
How would you tell the story?
Share your story with your class.

Teacher: Children use listening and speaking skills to share stories about themselves.

Name _____

 1 Getting Story Ideas

Sal wanted to write a story for
his classmates.
He wanted to tell them about
something he did.
First he drew a picture.
Talk about Sal's picture.

Try Your Hand

Think about something you have done.
Draw a picture about it.

COMPOSITION: PREWRITING   **Teacher:** Children draw pictures of their story ideas.

Adding Story Details

Sal looked at his picture.
He remembered other things he did.
Then Sal added more to his picture.
Talk about what Sal added.

Try Your Hand

Look at your story picture.
What can you add?

WRITING PROCESS

Teacher: Children discuss their pictures and add details.

2 ## Writing Your Story

Sal looked at his picture.
Then Sal wrote his story in order.

At the Beach

I went to the beach.
My dad took me. We
made a fort.

Try Your Hand

Look at your story picture.
Write a story that you can
share with your friends.
Write your story in order.

Who? Why? What?

WRITING PROCESS

Teacher: Children use their ideas to write their stories.

Name _____

COMPOSITION: DRAFTING

3 ## Adding to Your Story

Sal read aloud his story to Mary.
Mary asked Sal what happened next.
Sal added to his story.

At the Beach

I went to the beach.
My dad took me. We
made a fort. We swam.
                     ∧

Try Your Hand

Talk about your story
with a classmate.
What can you add?

Use this mark ∧.
Add to your story.
The water was icy cold.
∧
The water was icy cold.

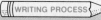 WRITING PROCESS

Teacher: Children discuss their stories
and add to them.

COMPOSITION: RESPONDING/REVISING

Checking Capital Letters

Sal read his story again.
He made sure each sentence began with
a capital letter.
Find the capital letters.

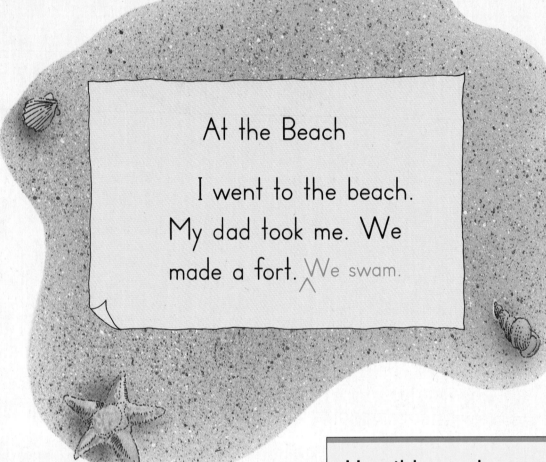

At the Beach

I went to the beach.
My dad took me. We
made a fort. We swam.

Try Your Hand

Read your story.
Check each sentence.
Make sure each sentence
begins with a capital letter.

Use this mark ☰ .
Show where a capital
letter goes.
i helped Dad.
☰
I helped Dad.

WRITING PROCESS

Teacher: Children check capital letters in their stories.

5 Sharing Your Story

Sal copied his story.
Sal and his class shared their stories and pictures.

Try Your Hand

Copy your story onto another piece of paper.
Share your story and your picture with a classmate.

WRITING PROCESS

Teacher: Children publish their stories.   COMPOSITION: PUBLISHING **87**

Writing in the Content Areas
Social Studies

People have special homes.
Draw a picture of your home.
Write a sentence about your home.
Tell how it is special.

Teacher: Children write or dictate sentences about their pictures.

Name _____

CONNECTING
WRITING AND LANGUAGE

Look for words that name people, places, and things in this story.

My dad and I go fishing.

We ride in a boat out to sea .

Sometimes we catch fish .

My dad is not a great fisherman .

He is a great dad !

The blue words name people, places, and things.
They are naming words.

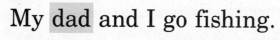

Name _____

◆ Some **naming words** name people.

worker

driver

mother

son

▶ Write each word that names
a person.

1. A driver is in the truck.

2. My son sees the dog.

3. The worker chases the dog.

driver

_____

_____

_____

Teacher: Children identify and write naming
words for people.

Name  _____

> ## THINK AND REMEMBER
> ◆ Use **naming words** to name people.

Practice

■ Finish each sentence.
You may use a word from the box.

> mother   worker   driver
> son   man

4. A <u>mother</u> walks.

5. Her _____ calls his dog.

6. The dog runs from the _____.

7. Now the _____ can move.

8. The _____ holds a flag.

Name _____

◆ Some **naming words** name animals.

cow

horse

cat

pig

duck

dog

goat

chick

▶ Draw a line under each word
that names an animal.

| 1. <u>dog</u> | 2. ruler | 3. goat | 4. cow | 5. pig |

Teacher: Children identify and write naming
words for animals.

Name _____

THINK AND REMEMBER
◆ Use **naming words** to name animals.

Practice

■ Write the naming word for the animal shown in each sentence.

6. Meg's is in the barn.

7. Joe feeds the .

8. What a pretty !

9. A  pecks the dirt.

10. The  moos.

11. Is the hungry?

12. My likes to play.

3 Naming Words for Places

◆ Some **naming words** name places.

▶ Draw a line under each word that names a place.

1. <u>town</u>   **2.** flower   **3.** house

4. father   **5.** sea   **6.** cat

Write the words that name places.

7.    8. _____   9. _____

Teacher: Children identify and write naming words for places.

THINK AND REMEMBER

◆ Use **naming words** to name places.

Practice

■ Write a naming word for each small picture.
The big picture will help you.

10.

park

11.

_____

12.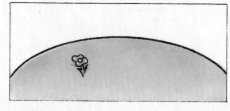

_____

13.

_____

14.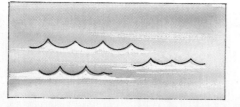

_____

Name _____

4 Naming Words for Things

◆ Some **naming words** name things.

Labels in illustration: window, star, chair, book, desk, crayon, paper, table

▶ Draw a line around each word that names a thing.

1. A boy reads at his (desk).

2. What is his book about?

3. Someone hangs a star.

4. It is pretty by the window.

Teacher: Children identify and write naming words for things.

Name _____

THINK AND REMEMBER
◆ Use **naming words** to name things.

Practice

■ Finish each sentence.
Use words from the box.

| table | crayon | chair | paper | picture |

5. One girl sits at a $\underline{\hspace{1cm}}$ table $\underline{\hspace{1cm}}$.

6. Her teacher sits on a $\underline{\hspace{3cm}}$.

7. He helps her draw a $\underline{\hspace{3cm}}$.

8. I color with a $\underline{\hspace{3cm}}$.

9. May I have more $\underline{\hspace{3cm}}$?

Name _____

5 | Naming More Than One

◆ Some **naming words** name more than one.

A naming word can name one. 😊 girl

A naming word can name more than one. 👧👧 girls

Some naming words add **s** to name more than one.

▶ Match the naming words and the pictures.

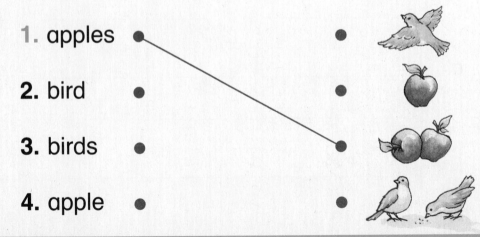

1. apples •

2. bird •

3. birds •

4. apple •

HBJ material copyrighted under notice appearing earlier in this work.

98 GRAMMAR/SPELLING

Teacher: Children identify and write naming words that name more than one.

Name _____

THINK AND REMEMBER

◆ Add <u>s</u> to make **naming words** name more than one.

Practice

■ Finish each sentence with a word from the picture.

5. Two  <u>girls</u> carry a ladder.

6. Let's climb these _____ .

7. The girls pick more _____ .

8. Three _____ are full.

9. Those _____ fly.

10. Do you eat _____ ?

11. The _____ have fun.

Building Vocabulary
Compound Words

butterfly

treehouse

backpack

notebook

campfire

tree + house = treehouse

Practice

Write the compound words.

1. camp + fire = campfire

2. butter + fly = _____

3. note + book = _____

Teacher: Children identify and write compound words.

Name _____

Poetry

Listen to this poem.
Read aloud the poem with classmates.

Things That Sing
by Charlotte Zolotow

Sing sing sing
crickets sing
birds sing
kettles sing
radiators sing
violins sing
leaves in trees sing
and sometimes mothers sing
           sing sing sing.

Teacher: Read aloud the poem. Children
participate in a choral reading.

Language Enrichment
Naming Words

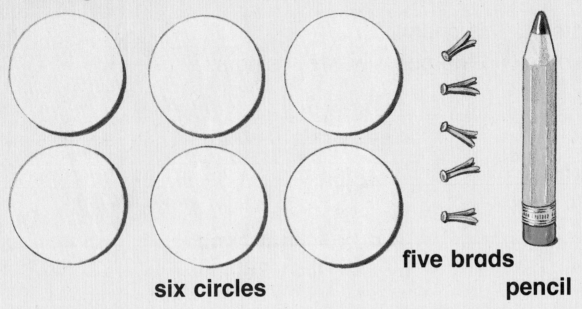

six circles

five brads

pencil

Wordy Worm

1. Write a naming word on five circles.
   Write some words that name more than one.
2. Draw a face for the worm on the last circle.
3. Put the words and the face together with brads.
4. Use the words in sentences.

Wordy Worm lives under a <u>rock</u>.

rock   boy   bugs   lake   trees

Teacher: Children make Wordy Worm and use nouns to generate sentences about it.

CONNECTING
LANGUAGE AND WRITING

kites   balloon

seagull

mother

boy   father   beach

dog

Write sentences about the picture.
Use the naming words in your sentences.

_____

- - - - - - - - - - - - - - - - -

_____

- - - - - - - - - - - - - - - - -

_____

- - - - - - - - - - - - - - - - -

_____

- - - - - - - - - - - - - - - - -

_____

- - - - - - - - - - - - - - - - -

_____

Teacher: Children write sentences
about the picture.

Name _____

2 Unit Checkup

Story About You   pages 77–79

Lee wrote this story.
Read the story and follow the directions.

In the Mountains

I went to the mountains. We visited a
park. A man gave us hats with lights.
We went into a cave. I learned about rocks.

---

1. Draw a line under the answer to the question.
What does Lee tell about herself?

a. She has a big family.   **b.** She went to a cave.

2. Write <u>first</u>, <u>next</u>, and <u>last</u> to put the pictures in order.

_____   _____   _____

Teacher: Read aloud the directions for each exercise.

Writing Process   pages 80–87

Lee added something to her story.
Then she made sure each sentence began
with a capital letter.
Draw a line around the part she added.
Draw a line under each capital letter.

3.

I saw some bats.

We went into a cave.∧I learned about rocks.

Naming Words for People   pages 90–91

Find each word that names a person.
Then write the word.

4. The girl plays.   _____

5. Her father rides.   _____

Naming Words for Animals   pages 92–93

Draw a line under each word that names an animal.

6. fox   **7.** house   **8.** lion   **9.** kitten

Name _____

Naming Words for Places and Things   pages 94–97

Draw a line under each word that names a place.

10. beach   **11.** chair   **12.** park

13. book   **14.** town   **15.** sea

Look at the words above.
Write the words that name things.

_____   _____

16. _____   **17.** _____

Naming More Than One   pages 98–99

Finish each sentence.
Write the word that names more than one.

(girl, girls)
_____

18. The _____ have kites.

(birds, bird)
_____

19. Many _____ fly.

(tree, trees)
_____

20. Two _____ are tall.

UNIT

3

Sharing Your News

◆ COMPOSITION FOCUS: Friendly Letter
◆ LANGUAGE FOCUS: Special Naming Words

Teacher: Children discuss the photograph.

Reading with a Writer's Eye

Listen to Ebony's letter.
Talk about what it says.

October 24, 1990

Dear James,

   Yesterday my class went to the Aquarium. We saw a gray stingray and a starfish.
We also saw sea otters. You would like the sea otters.
They are fun to watch. I made a bookmark for you. I hope you like it.

Your friend,

Ebony

Teacher: Read the letters. Children discuss the content and purpose of each one.

Listen to James's thank-you letter.
Talk about what it says.

November 1, 1990

Dear Ebony,

Thank you for the red
bookmark with the starfish
and the shells. I will
use it when I read. It will
save my place.

Your friend,

James

Name _____

Listen to Ebony's invitation.
Talk about what it says.

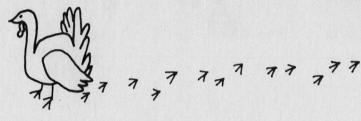

November 10, 1990

Dear James,

Would you like to come
to my Thanksgiving feast?
I will help make a turkey, some
brown beans, a pie, and some
warm tea. Please come at
4:00 in the afternoon.

Your friend,

Ebony

Thinking As a Writer
Studying a Friendly Letter

A **friendly letter** is written to someone you know.
It tells something about yourself.
A friendly letter has five parts.
Look at the five parts in Ebony's letter.

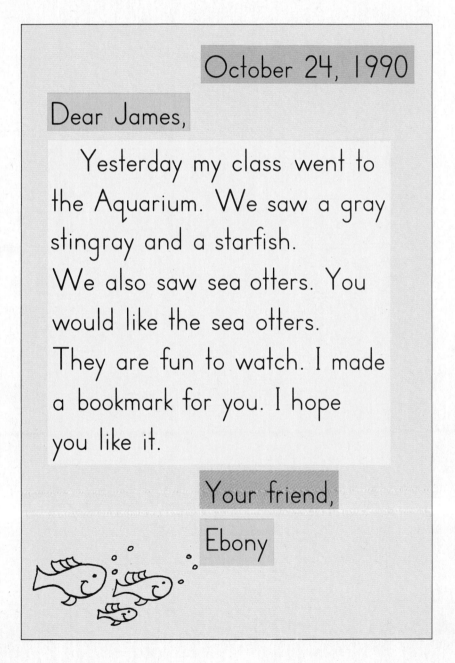

October 24, 1990

Dear James,

   Yesterday my class went to the Aquarium. We saw a gray stingray and a starfish.
We also saw sea otters. You would like the sea otters.
They are fun to watch. I made a bookmark for you. I hope you like it.

Your friend,

Ebony

Teacher: Children discuss and identify
the parts of the letter.

Thinking As a Writer
Picturing Events

Ebony wanted to write a letter to James.
First she thought about what she saw at
the Aquarium.
She remembered what she did.

What do you think Ebony did next?
Draw a picture to show what happens.

Teacher: Children discuss the pictures and
draw pictures to show what happens next.

Listening and Speaking
Giving Your Opinion

Clarence buys a present for his friend Robert.
He wants to give Robert a key ring.
His sister has another idea.
What do you think she says to Clarence?
Why?

Pretend you are in the picture.
What would you say to Clarence?

Teacher: Children use persuasion to discuss the picture.

1 Getting Ideas for a Letter

Mickey wanted to write a letter to her friend Mr. Willis.
She wanted to tell Mr. Willis something about herself.
First, she made a list of ideas.
Then, she chose one idea.

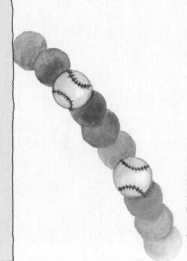

ideas for a letter

my new bike
my home run
my birthday party

Try Your Hand

Think about writing a letter to a friend.
What can you tell about yourself?
Make a list of your ideas.
Choose one idea to write about.

WRITING PROCESS

Teacher: Children list ideas for their friendly letters.

Adding Details

Mickey thought about her baseball game.
She closed her eyes and saw again
what happened.
She made a list of things she saw.

<u>my home run</u>

hit the ball
ran fast
Billy dropped the ball
ran to home plate

Try Your Hand

Think about your idea.
Close your eyes and try to see what happened.
Make a list of the things you see.

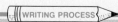 WRITING PROCESS

2 Writing a Friendly Letter

Mickey looked at her list.
Then she wrote her letter.

May 25, 1990

Dear Mr. Willis,

   I made a home run. I hit the ball
and ran fast. Billy caught the ball
and dropped it. Then I ran to home
plate. It was a great game!

           Your friend,

           Mickey

Try Your Hand

Look at your list.
Write a letter to your friend.

Who? Why?
What?

WRITING PROCESS

Teacher: Children use their lists to write friendly letters.

Name _____

Teacher: Children write their first drafts.

COMPOSITION: DRAFTING **117**

Name _____

WRITING PROCESS

3 Adding to Your Letter

Mickey read her letter to Pete.
They talked about it.
Mickey added another sentence.

May 25, 1990

Dear Mr. Willis,

    I made a home run. I hit the ball
and ran fast. Billy caught the ball
and dropped it. Then I ran to home
Everyone cheered!
plate. ∧ It was a great game!

Your friend,
Mickey

Try Your Hand

Talk about your letter
with a classmate.
What can you add?

Use this mark ∧.
Add to your letter.

    great
I have ∧ news!
I have great news!

WRITING PROCESS

Teacher: Children discuss their
letters and add to them.

COMPOSITION: RESPONDING/REVISING **119**

Name _____

4 Checking Capital Letters and End Marks

Mickey checked the capital letter at the beginning
of each sentence.
She checked the end marks.
Find the capital letters and end marks in Mickey's letter.

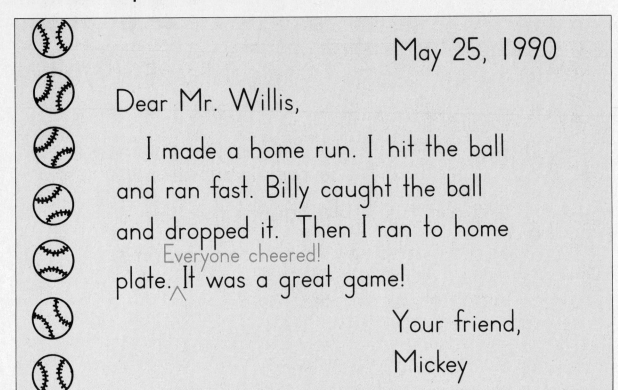

May 25, 1990

Dear Mr. Willis,

   I made a home run. I hit the ball
and ran fast. Billy caught the ball
and dropped it. Then I ran to home
plate. It was a great game!
        Everyone cheered!

                    Your friend,
                    Mickey

Try Your Hand

Make sure each sentence
begins with a capital letter.
Check the end mark in each
sentence.

Use this mark ⫪.
Show where a capital
letter goes.

we play games.
‗‗

We play games.

Teacher: Children identify and use capital
letters and end marks in their letters.

5 **Mailing Your Letter**

Mickey copied her letter.
She wrote Mr. Willis's address on an envelope.

Mickey Landis
245 Wilton Road
Dayton, Ohio 45390

Mr. Don Willis
2937 River Road
Albany, New York 12201

Then Mickey put the letter in the envelope and mailed it.

Try Your Hand

Copy your letter.
Write your friend's address
on an envelope.
Add a stamp.
Then mail the letter.

WRITING PROCESS

Teacher: Children mail their letters.

Writing in the Content Areas
Language Arts

Some storybook characters are like friends.
Write a letter to a storybook character.
Tell why you like him or her.
Then tell something interesting about yourself.
Share your letter with a classmate.

Teacher: Children write or dictate letters to storybook characters.

CONNECTING
WRITING AND LANGUAGE

Look for words that name people, places, days, and months in this letter.

April 30, 1990

Dear Rosie,

   On Sunday I marched in the Hartford parade. Mom made a butterfly costume for me. It had yellow wings.

         Love,
         Lucy

The blue words name people, places, days, and months. They are special naming words.

Teacher: Children identify the special naming words in the letter.

Name _____

1 Naming Words for Special People and Animals

◆ Some **naming words** name special people and animals.

Jim   Zip   Brownie   Flip   Pip   Lisa

The names of people and animals begin with capital letters.

 Jim   Brownie

▶ Draw a line under the names of people and animals.

1. <u>Lisa</u>	**2.** dog	**3.** Flip	**4.** Jim	**5.** girl

Teacher: Children identify and write the names of people and animals.

THINK AND REMEMBER

◆ Begin names of special people and animals with capital letters.

Practice

■ Finish each sentence.
Write the name of a person or an animal.

6.  Lisa _____ names each puppy.

7. She sees _____ roll over.

8. _____ is the little one.

9. The sleepy one is _____

10. _____ has a white spot.

11. _____ pets the dog.

Application: See the *Teacher's Edition.*   GRAMMAR/MECHANICS **125**

2 Naming Words for Special Places

◆ Some **naming words** name special places.

The names of special places begin with capital letters.

Pine **S**treet   **T**exas

▶ Draw a line around the names of special places.

1. Ana lives in Logan City.   2. The city is in Utah.

3. Oak School is big.   4. Pine Street is here.

5. Where is Texas?   6. I live on Ash Road.

Teacher: Children identify and write the names of special places.

Name _____

THINK AND REMEMBER
◆ Begin names of special places with capital letters.

My Special Places

Practice

■ Finish each sentence. Write the name of your own special place.

7. I live in the town of _____

_____

_____.

8. The name of my state is _____

_____

_____.

9. The street where I live is _____

_____

_____.

Name _____

◆ Some **naming words** name the days of the week.

Sunday
Monday
Tuesday
Wednesday
Thursday
Friday
Saturday

We go to school on Monday .

The names of the days of the week begin with capital letters.

On Tuesday we paint pictures.

▶ Draw a line under each day of the week that is written correctly.

1. Brian goes to the library on (Wednesday, wednesday).

2. On (Thursday, thursday) our class writes stories.

3. On (friday, Friday) I play baseball.

Teacher: Children identify and write the names of the days of the week.

Name _____

THINK AND REMEMBER

◆ Begin the names of the days of the week with capital letters.

Practice

■ On what days do you go to school? Write the names of the days.

We play ball on Saturday.

4. Monday

5. _____

6. _____

7. _____

8. _____

Name _____

◆ Some **naming words** name the months of the year.

January
February
March

April
May
June

July
August
September

October
November
December

The names of the months of the year begin with capital letters.

It is windy in Ó October.

▶ Draw a line under each word that names a month.

1. Pink flowers grow in April.

2. June is warm.

3. We pick cherries in July.

Write the words.

4. April   5. _____   6. _____

Teacher: Children identify and write the names of the months of the year.

Name _____

THINK AND REMEMBER

◆ Begin the names of the months of the
year with capital letters.

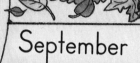

September

Practice

■ Finish each sentence.
Write the name of a month.

7. In ___September___ school begins.

8. Last month was _____.

9. This month is _____.

10. Next month will be _____.

11. My birthday is in _____.

Application: See the *Teacher's Edition.*

Name _____

◆ The words he, she, and it take the place of some naming words.

The word He takes the place of the name Ross.

Ross sits and looks.

He sits and looks.

▶ Finish each sentence. Write He, She, or It.

The bike

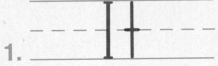

1. _____ is new.

Lori

_____

2. _____ rides well.

Dad

_____

3. _____ is proud.

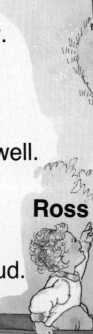

Dad

Lori

bike

Mom

Ross

wagon

Teacher: Children identify and write the words he, she, and it.

Name _____

THINK AND REMEMBER

◆ Use <u>he</u>, <u>she</u>, and <u>it</u> to take the place of some naming words.

Practice

■ Write a word from the box that can take the place of the naming word.

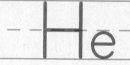

He	She	It

4. Ross is too small for a bike.

He

5. The wagon is red.

_____

6. Mom pulls the wagon.

_____

7. This bike is mine.

_____

8. Dad takes a picture.

_____

Name _____

◆ The words I and me take the place of some naming words.

Use I in the naming part of a sentence.

1. **I** am seven today.

Use me in the telling part of a sentence.

2. Mom gives me a party.

▶ Draw a line around the word that belongs in the sentence.

1. ____ invite my friends.   I   me

2. Mom shows ____ the cake.   I   me

3. My friends sing ____ a song.   I   me

4. ____ blow out the candles.   I   me

Teacher: Children identify and write the words I and me.

THINK AND REMEMBER

◆ Use <u>I</u> and <u>me</u> to take the place of your name.

Practice

■ Finish each sentence.
Write <u>I</u> or <u>me</u>.

(I, me)

5. _____ <u>I</u> _____ share the cake.

(I, me)

6. Ken gives _____ a special present.

(I, me)

7. _____ thank him for the kite.

(I, me)

8. Tina hands _____ a pretty card.

(I, me)

9. _____ think this is a great party!

Building Vocabulary
Words That Sound Alike

Read the sentences in the picture.

I am four . The apple is for me.

Mary is two . Give the banana to Mary.

Some words sound alike but have different spellings. Which words sound alike?

Practice

■ Draw a line around the word that goes with each picture.

1.   dear
        deer

2.   I
        eye

3.   two
        to

4.    hear
        here

Teacher: Children choose correct words for the pictures.

Listening and Speaking

Poetry

Listen to the poem.
Then read aloud the poem with your class.

My Sister Laura
by Spike Milligan

My sister Laura's bigger than me
And lifts me up quite easily.
I can't lift her, I've tried and tried;
She must have something heavy inside.

Teacher: Read aloud the poem. Children participate in a choral reading.

LISTENING AND SPEAKING **137**

Language Enrichment
Special Naming Words

I am Tanya .
Spot is my dragon.
We went to New York
in a little red wagon.

He went, she went, we all went away,
In the month of March on a Saturday !

Name Game

Read Tanya's poem.

The blue words are special naming words.

Make up another verse for the poem.

Use your own special naming words.

Take turns sharing your poems.

Teacher: Children complete poems.

Name _____

CONNECTING
LANGUAGE AND WRITING

Third Street
sign
Neil
street
Mom
building
Marc

Write sentences about the picture.
Use special names for the people and places.

_____
- -
_____
_____
- -
_____
_____
- -
_____
_____
- -
_____

Teacher: Children write sentences
about the picture.

3 Unit Checkup

Friendly Letter   pages 111–112

Sue wrote a letter to her friend Ann.
Read the letter and follow the directions.

> November 2, 1990
>
> Dear Ann,
>
>   Last week I started dancing lessons. I have new shoes. They have taps on the heels and the toes. They make a lot of noise!
>
>   Your friend,
>   Sue

1. Draw a line under the answer to the question. Which part tells who will get the letter?

   a. Your friend,   **b.** Dear Ann,

2. Draw a line around the picture that shows what Sue wrote about.

Teacher: Read aloud the directions for each exercise.

Writing Process   pages 114–121

Sue added a sentence to her letter.

> <u>my</u> shoes are black.

3. Draw a line under the answer to the question.
What did Sue correct in her sentence?

a. an end mark   **b.** a capital letter

Naming Words for Special People, Animals, and Places   pages 124–127

Draw a line under the names of people and animals.

4. My name is Ken.   **5.** Jan is my sister.

6. We live in Rivertown.   **7.** Rascal is our dog.

Write the word that names a special place.

8. _____

Days of the Week and Months of the Year
pages 128–131

Draw a line under the month or day that
is written correctly.

9. The flowers bloom in (june, June).

10. On (friday, Friday) we water the garden.

Name _____

Finish each sentence.
Write He, She, or It.

11. _____ digs a hole.

                ― ― ― ― ― ― ―

12. _____ will grow.

                ― ― ― ― ― ― ―

13. _____ helps.

                ― ― ― ― ― ― ―

14. _____ likes the tree.

Using I and Me   pages 134–135

Draw a line around the word that belongs
in the sentence.

15. Dad asks ___ about school.   I   me

16. ___ tell him.   I   me

17. ___ can sing a song.   I   me

18. He gives ___ a hug.   I   me

UNIT

4

Building Rhymes

◆ **COMPOSITION FOCUS:** Poem
◆ **LANGUAGE FOCUS:** Action Words

by the bay, where the watermelons grow
to my home I dare not
I do my mother will say

Bb   Cc   Ff Gg   H

Teacher: Children discuss the photograph.

UNIT 4   **143**

HBJ material copyrighted under notice appearing earlier in this work.

Name _____

Reading with a Writer's Eye

Listen to the poem.
Then read the poem with your class.

Down by the Bay
Adapted by Raffi

Down by the bay, where the watermelons grow,
Back to my home I dare not go.
For if I do my mother will say,
"Did you ever see a goose kissing a moose,
Down by the bay?"

Teacher: Read aloud the poem. Children participate in a choral reading.

Down by the bay, where the watermelons grow,
Back to my home I dare not go.
For if I do my mother will say,
"Did you ever see a whale with a polka-dot tail,
Down by the bay?"

Thinking As a Writer
Studying a Poem

"Down by the Bay" is a **poem.**
This poem has words that sound alike.
These words are **rhyming words.**
Listen to the rhyming words in the poem.

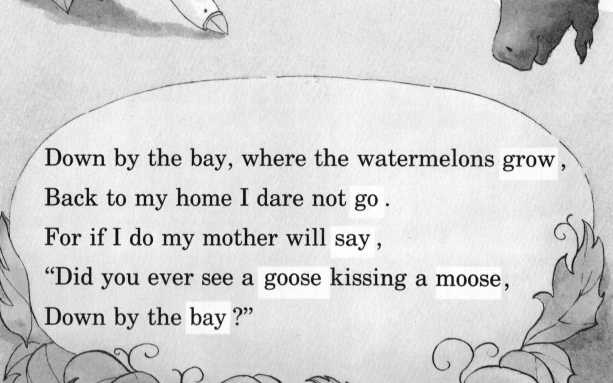

Down by the bay, where the watermelons grow,

Back to my home I dare not go.

For if I do my mother will say,

"Did you ever see a goose kissing a moose,

Down by the bay?"

Teacher: Read aloud the poem and help
children identify the rhyming words.

Thinking As a Writer
Seeing Patterns

Many poems have **word patterns.**
Word patterns are groups of words
that rhyme or sound alike.

> a <u>pig</u> wearing a <u>wig</u>
>
> a <u>goose</u> kissing a <u>moose</u>

Finish the word patterns.
Use words from the box.

> mail   mouse   fly   hole

1. a snail reading its _____ mail _____

2. a _____ wearing a tie

3. a mole digging a _____

4. a _____ cleaning its house

Listening and Speaking
Sharing Ideas

These children are making something.
They have many good ideas.
How do they share their ideas?

How do you share your ideas with your class?
Talk about ways you do things together.

Teacher: Children discuss sharing ideas.

1 Getting Ideas for a Poem

Sarah wanted to write a poem for other children.
She looked at the word pattern in the poem.

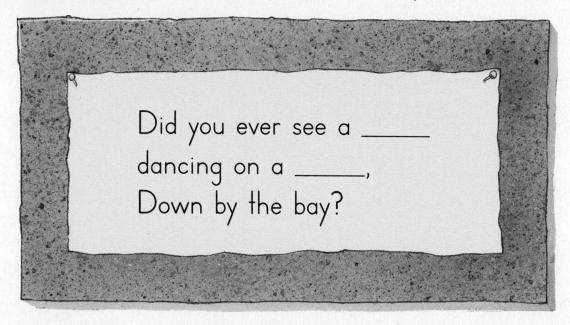

Did you ever see a _____
dancing on a _____,
Down by the bay?

Then, she made a list of rhyming words.

1. cat   mat
2. duck   truck
3. bug   jug

⌦ WRITING PROCESS ⟩

Teacher: Children discuss rhyming words.   COMPOSITION: PREWRITING **149**

Try Your Hand

Look at the word pattern.
Make a list of rhyming words to fit the word pattern.

> Did you ever see a _____
> dancing on a _____,
> Down by the bay?

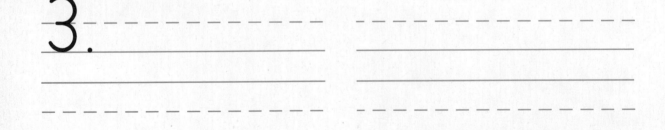

WRITING PROCESS

Teacher: Children generate rhyming words for poems.

Choosing Rhyming Words

Sarah looked at the rhyming words.
She chose two rhyming words.
She drew a line around each word.

Try Your Hand

Look at your list of rhyming words.
Draw a line around the words you want to use
in your poem.

WRITING PROCESS
Teacher: Children choose a pair of rhyming words
to use in their poems.

COMPOSITION: PREWRITING **151**

Name _____

2 Writing a Poem

Sarah wrote her poem.
She used her rhyming words.

Did you ever see a funny duck
dancing on a truck
Down by the bay?

Try Your Hand

Write your poem for other children.
Use your rhyming words.

Who?
What? Why?

HBJ material copyrighted under notice appearing earlier in this work.

WRITING PROCESS

152 COMPOSITION: DRAFTING   **Teacher:** Children use rhyming words to write poems.

WRITING PROCESS

3 Making Changes

Sarah read her poem to Juan.
They talked about what she
could change.
Sarah took out one word.
Now her poem fits the pattern.

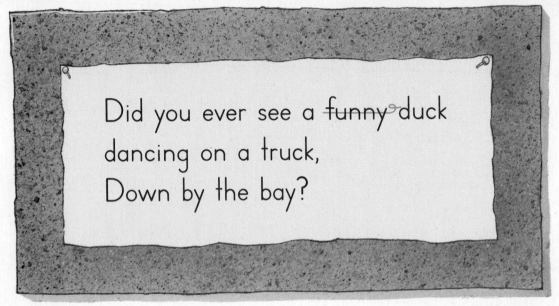

Did you ever see a ~~funny~~ duck
dancing on a truck,
Down by the bay?

Try Your Hand

Talk about your poem with a classmate.
Does your poem fit the word pattern?
What words can you take away?

Use this mark ——⸲ to take away a word.
Did you ever see a ~~lazy~~ cat?
Did you ever see a cat?

WRITING PROCESS

Teacher: Children discuss and
revise their poems.

Sharing Your Poem

Sarah copied her poem.
Her class made mobiles of their poems.

Down by the bay where the watermelons grow,
Back to my home I dare not go.
For if I do my mother will say,

Did you ever see a duck

dancing on a truck,
Down by the bay?

Try Your Hand

Make a copy of your poem.
Think of a way to share it with other children.

WRITING PROCESS

Teacher: Children publish their poems.   COMPOSITION: PUBLISHING **155**

Writing in the Content Areas
Music

Look at the word pattern in this song.
Finish the song and sing it with your class.

> Ride, ride, ride your bike
> Quickly down the street!
> When you see a traffic light
>
> _____
>
> \- \- \- \- \- \- \- \-
>
> Stop on your two _____!

Here is another verse for the song.
Finish the song and share it with your class.

> Sing, sing, sing a song
>
> _____
>
> \- \- \- \- \- \- \- \-
>
> Sweetly as can _____!
>
> I can sing my ABC's
>
> _____
>
> \- \- \- \- \- \- \- \-
>
> Won't you sing with _____?

Make up other verses for the song.
Use the word pattern.

Teacher: Children write original words for a song.

CONNECTING
WRITING AND LANGUAGE

You wrote a poem about an animal.
What does this poem tell about an animal?

Giraffes Don't Huff
by Karla Kuskin

Giraffes don't huff or hoot or howl
They never grump, they never growl
They never roar, they never riot,
They eat green leaves
And just keep quiet.

The blue words tell about an animal.
They are action words.
You will learn about action words.

Teacher: Children identify the action words in the poem.

1 Action Words

◆ An **action word** tells what someone or something does.

points

climbs

jumps

digs

rolls

rakes

▶ Write the action word in each sentence.

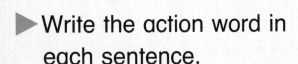

1. Myra points to the kittens.

points

2. Carl turns around.

_____

3. They laugh at the kittens.

_____

Teacher: Children identify and write action words.

Name _____

THINK AND REMEMBER

◆ Use an **action word** to tell what someone or something does.

Practice

■ Finish each sentence with an action word.
The big picture will help you.

4. The kittens __play__ with us.

5. Jet _____ up a tree.

6. Pumpkin _____ down.

7. Smoky _____ over.

8. Snowy _____ a hole.

Name _____

◆ An **action word** can tell about now.

Mom <u>claps</u>.

Rob and Doug <u>race</u>.

▶ Write each action word.

1. Rob hops on one foot.

hops

2. Doug jumps up and down.

3. Both boys move quickly.

Teacher: Children identify and write present-tense action words.

Name _____

THINK AND REMEMBER
◆ Some **action words** tell about now.

Practice

■ Finish each sentence
with an action word.
Use the words from the box.

grabs	barks	runs
	chase	catch

4. Ruff 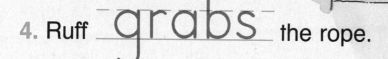 the rope.

5. Then Ruff _____ away.

6. The boys _____ the dog.

7. Ruff _____ loudly.

8. Do they _____ the dog?

Name _____

3 | Adding s to Action Words

◆ An s is added to some **action words** that tell about now.

falls

claps

hops

climbs

Some action words that tell about one end with s.

1. One hat falls off.

Action words that tell about more than one do not end in s.

2. Two hats fall off.

▶ Draw a line under the action words that tell about one.

1. A boy <u>claps</u> his hands.   2. The frog hops.

3. The girls laugh.   4. The children play.

Teacher: Children identify and write action words that tell about one and more than one.

Name _____

THINK AND REMEMBER

◆ Add an <u>s</u> to some **action words** that tell about now.

Practice

■ Finish each sentence.
Write the correct action word.

(climb, climbs)

5. Mr. Darrow ___climbs___ a ladder.

(join, joins)

6. Three girls _____ hands.

(dance, dances)

7. They _____ in a row.

(sing, sings)

8. Mae _____ a silly song.

Name _____

4 Action Words About the Past

◆ An **action word** can tell about the past.

jumped

laughed

kicked

Some action words tell about the past.
Some end with <u>ed</u>.

Cappy walk<u>ed</u> in a funny way.

▶ Draw a line under the action words that tell about the past.

1. Cappy (<u>jumped</u>, jumps) up and down.

2. He (laughs, laughed) at a joke.

3. Cappy (kicked, kicks) one leg.

Teacher: Children identify and write past-tense action words.

Name _____

THINK AND REMEMBER
◆ Add <u>ed</u> to some **action words** to tell about the past.

Practice
■ Write sentences that tell about the past. The pictures will help you.

rolled

painted

shouted

rested

4. _____

_____

5. _____

_____

6. _____

_____

7. _____

5 Using Is and Are

◆ The words <u>is</u> and <u>are</u> tell about now.

This <u>is</u> a funny hat.

Both hats <u>are</u> funny.

Use <u>is</u> to tell about one person, place, or thing.

1. The show is funny.

Use <u>are</u> to tell about more than one person, place, or thing.

2. Those puppets are silly.

▶ Fill in the circles.
Show how many the blue words tell about.

1. One hat is big.   one ●   more than one ○

2. This hat is small.   one ○   more than one ○

3. The hats are mixed up.   one ○   more than one ○

Teacher: Children identify and write correct verb forms.

Name  _____

THINK AND REMEMBER

◆ Use <u>is</u> to tell about one.

◆ Use <u>are</u> to tell about more than one.

Practice

■ Finish each sentence.
Write <u>is</u> or <u>are</u>.

4. The puppets ___are___ in the shop.

5. This hat _____ pink.

6. Her hat _____ blue.

7. Now they _____ happy.

8. The puppet _____ helpful.

9. The hats _____ fine.

6 | Using Was and Were

◆ The words <u>was</u> and <u>were</u> tell about the past.

Use <u>was</u> to tell about
one person, place, or thing.

1. <u>Koko</u> was surprised.

Use <u>were</u> to tell about more than
one person, place, or thing.

2. <u>All the bananas</u> were gone!

Pickles

Koko

▶ Finish each sentence.
Draw a line around <u>was</u> or <u>were</u>.

1. The bag ___ on Koko's back.   was   were

2. Some bananas ___ in the bag.   was   were

3. Then the bag ___ empty!   was   were

Name _____

THINK AND REMEMBER
◆ Use <u>was</u> to tell about one.
◆ Use <u>were</u> to tell about more than one.

Practice

■ Finish each sentence.
Write <u>was</u> or <u>were</u>.

4. The monkeys **were** in a tree.

5. They _____ hungry.

6. Koko _____ nearby.

7. Both bags _____ open.

8. That monkey _____ quick!

9. Koko _____ hungry too!

Name _____

◆ A **contraction** is a short way to write two words.

Use this mark **'** to make a contraction.

The special mark **'** takes the place of
the missing letter or letters.

are + not = aren't		do + not = don't
have + not = haven't		is + not = isn't

▶ Match the words and their contractions.

1. have not ●   ● aren't

2. do not ●   ● haven't

3. is not ●   ● don't

4. are not ●   ● isn't

Teacher: Children identify and write contractions.

Name _____

THINK AND REMEMBER

◆ Use a **contraction** to write two words in a shorter way.

◆ Use a special mark ' to take the place of missing letters.

Practice

■ Finish each sentence in the poem. Write a contraction.

do not

5. Please ___don't___ forget!

have not

6. We _____ stopped yet.

are not

7. Our jobs _____ through.

is not

8. The work _____ hard to do.

Name _____

Building Vocabulary
Words That Mean the Opposite

big

little

up

down

Opposites are words that have different meanings.

1. The giraffe is wet .

2. The mouse stays dry .

Practice

■ Match the opposites.
The pictures will help you.

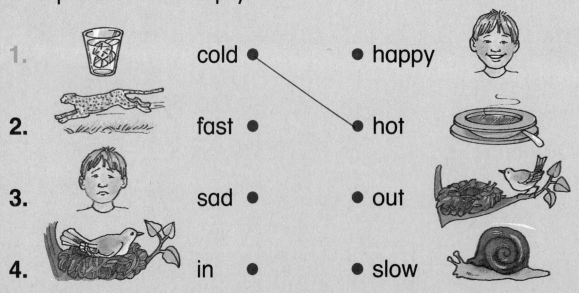

1. cold •   • happy

2. fast •   • hot

3. sad •   • out

4. in •   • slow

Teacher: Children match the opposites.

Listening and Speaking

Poetry

Listen to this poem.
Then do the actions with your class.

Wide Awake

by
Myra Cohn Livingston

I have to jump up
    out of bed
    and stretch my hands
    and rub my head,
    and curl my toes
    and yawn
    and shake
    myself
    all wide-awake!

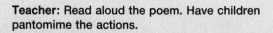

Teacher: Read aloud the poem. Have children
pantomime the actions.

Language Enrichment
Action Words

Action Word Dance

1. Think of actions you can do.
2. Share the action words with your class.
3. Write your words on the chalkboard.
4. Listen to dance music.
5. Move as your teacher calls out the action words.

Teacher: Children use action words and music to create a dance.

Name _____

CONNECTING
LANGUAGE AND WRITING

**Frog Pond
No Swimming!**

Little Bear

Big Bear

Word Bank

Now	Past
is	was
are	were
jump	jumped

Write sentences that tell about the bears.
Use the action words in the Word Bank.

_____

- -

_____

- -

_____

- -

_____

Teacher: Children write sentences
about the picture.

4 Unit Checkup

Poem   pages 146–147

Read Sam's poem and follow the directions.

> When you lie in bed,
> Can you see pictures in your head?
> Can you see a goat
> Riding on a boat?

1. Draw a line under the words that rhyme.

   a. bed, head   **b.** see, can

2. Finish the word pattern.
Write the missing word.

| dog   bee |

_____

a _____ buzzing around a tree

Writing Process   pages 149–155

Sam took out a word in another part of his poem.
Draw a line around the word he took out.

3.

> Can you see a silly hen
> Writing with a pen?

Teacher: Read aloud the directions for each exercise.

Name _____

Action Words About Now   pages 158–161

Write the action word in each sentence.

_____
- - - - - - - - - - - - -
4. The boys play ball.   _____

_____
- - - - - - - - - - - - -
5. The dog runs.   _____

_____
- - - - - - - - - - - - -
6. They call the dog.   _____

Adding s to Action Words   pages 162–163

Draw a line around the action word that tells about one.

7. Our teacher sings.   **8.** Pam and Ed sing.

Action Words About the Past   pages 164–165

Make each sentence tell about the past.
Draw a line under the correct word.

9. The clowns (paint, painted) a wall.

10. The paint (spilled, spills).

11. Jeff and Meg (laugh, laughed).

Name _____

Using Is and Are   pages 166–167

Finish each sentence.
Write is or are.

_____

12. These books _____ good.

_____

13. The joke _____ funny.

Using Was and Were   pages 168–169

Finish each sentence.
Draw a line under was or were.

14. The flowers (was, were) red.

15. That rose (was, were) pretty.

16. The flowers (was, were) on the table.

Contractions with Not   pages 170–171

Write the contractions for the words below.

are not   have not
_____   _____

17. _____   **18.** _____

is not   do not
_____   _____

19. _____   **20.** _____

Telling What Things Are Like

◆ **COMPOSITION FOCUS:** Description
◆ **LANGUAGE FOCUS:** Describing Words

Teacher: Children discuss the photograph.

Reading with a Writer's Eye

Listen to the information about pandas.
Tell about pandas.

from A Book About Pandas
by Ruth Belov Gross

_____

- -

_____

- -

_____

- -

_____

- -

Teacher: Read the description in the *Teacher's Edition.*
Children dictate or write sentences to retell it.

Thinking As a Writer
Studying a Description

Read part of the description of giant pandas.
What does the description tell about giant pandas?

Giant pandas are furry and fat. They look like great big teddy bears, only they are not brown like teddy bears. They are black and white.

Their legs are black. Their shoulders are black. Their ears are black, and the fur around their black eyes is black too.

Teacher: Read and discuss
the description with children.

READING ↔ WRITING CONNECTION

Thinking As a Writer
Seeing Details

What does a panda look like?
Draw a line around the words that
describe a panda.

soft   little   black and white

blue   small ears   short tail

big   square   furry

Draw your own picture of a panda.

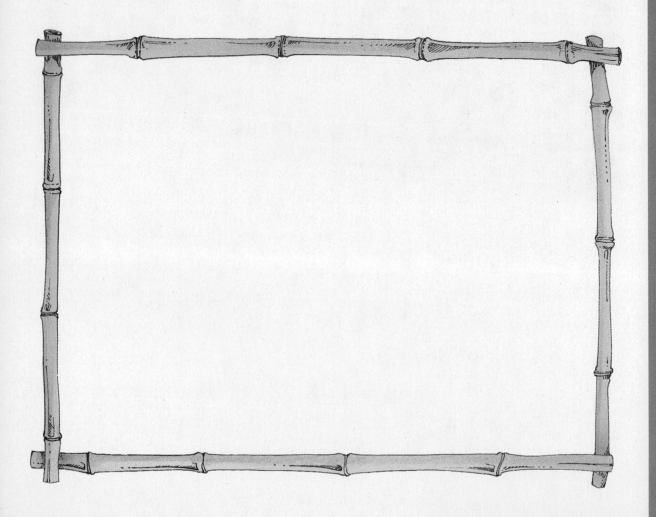

HBJ material copyrighted under notice appearing earlier in this work.

Teacher: Children identify
describing words and draw pictures.

Listening and Speaking
Giving a Description

Look closely at the picture.
What do you see?

Tell a classmate about the snake in the picture.

Name _____

Mrs. Li's class wanted to write a description for others
at school to read.
First they thought about places they had visited.
Then the class made a list.
They chose one place.

Try Your Hand

Think of things your class has seen.
Make a list.
Choose one idea to write about.

WRITING PROCESS

Teacher: Children make a list of ideas for a description.

Organizing Information

Mrs. Li's class talked about their visit to Magee's Farm.
They remembered what it was like.
They made a drawing.

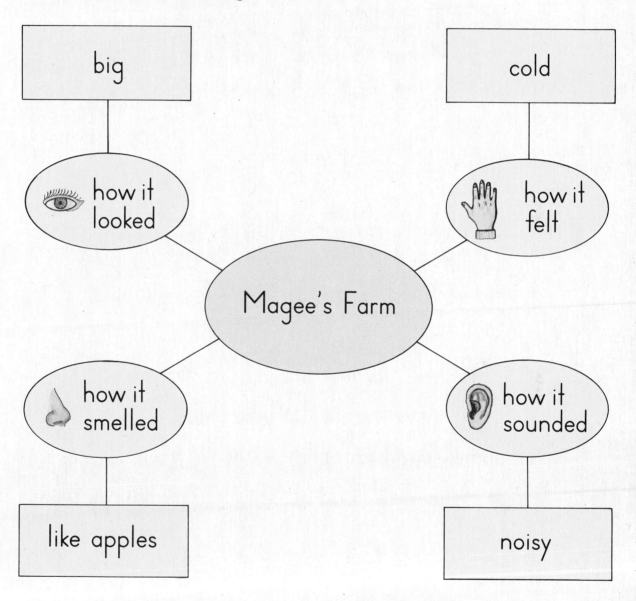

Try Your Hand

Think about your idea for a description.
Make a drawing showing words you want to use.

WRITING PROCESS

Teacher: Children generate details for a description.   COMPOSITION: PREWRITING **187**

2 Writing a Description

Mrs. Li's class used the drawing to write their description.

Magee's Farm

Magee's Farm is a big place. The workers there make apple cider. It was cold out that day. We heard the noisy machines press the apples. We could smell apples everywhere! We tasted some sweet cider.

Try Your Hand

Read your drawing. Then write a description to share with other children at your school.

Who? Why? What?

WRITING PROCESS

Teacher: Children use their ideas to dictate a description.

Name _____

3 Changing Details

The class talked about their description.
They changed a word to add
more details.

Magee's Farm

apple orchard

Magee's Farm is a big ⌃ place.
The workers there make apple
cider. It was cold out that day.
We heard the noisy machines
press the apples. We could smell
apples everywhere! We tasted
some sweet cider.

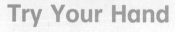

Try Your Hand

Read aloud your
class description.
What can you
change?

Use this mark ⌃ to change a word.

tons
We saw ⌃ ~~lots~~ of apples!
We saw tons of apples!

Teacher: Children discuss their description
and revise it.

COMPOSITION: RESPONDING/REVISING

Name ______________________________

4 Sharing Your Description

Mrs. Li's class made their description into a class mural.

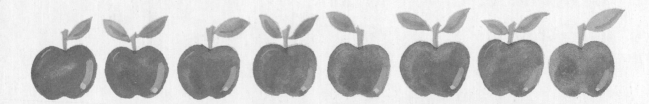

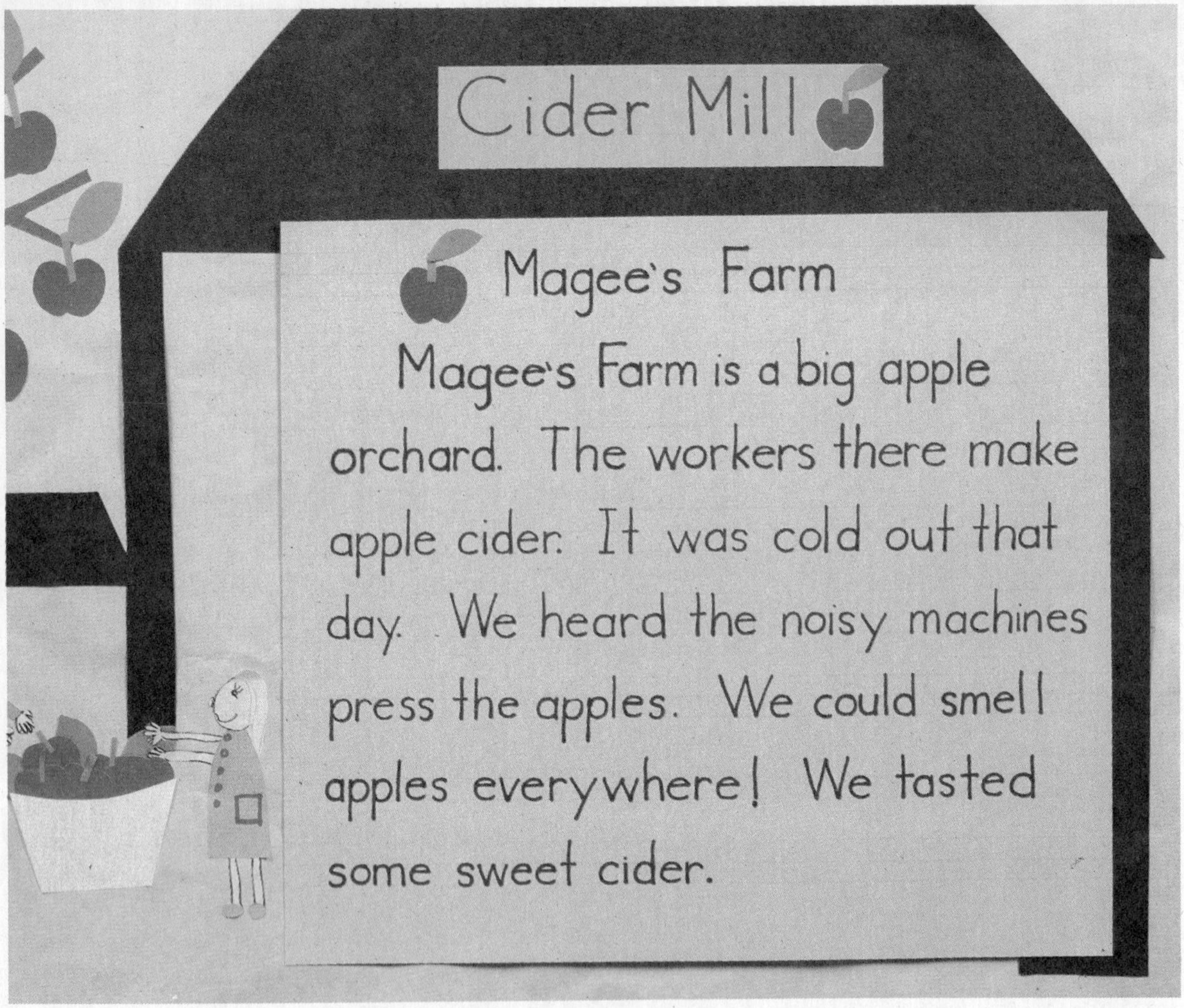
Cider Mill
Magee's Farm
Magee's Farm is a big apple orchard. The workers there make apple cider. It was cold out that day. We heard the noisy machines press the apples. We could smell apples everywhere! We tasted some sweet cider.

HBJ material copyrighted under notice appearing earlier in this work.

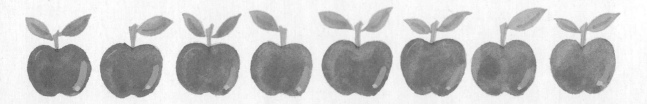

Teacher: Children publish their description.

The class shared their description with the whole school.

Try Your Hand

Make a copy of your description.
Share your description with another class.

Writing in the Content Areas
Social Studies/Art

Think about ways people travel.
How do you like to travel?
Make a stick picture.

1. Draw a picture of something you like
to ride in.
Cut out the picture.

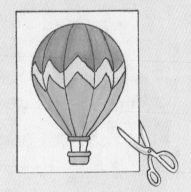

2. Write sentences that describe your
picture.

3. Glue the sentences to the back of
the picture.

4. Glue a stick to the picture.

5. Share your sentences and your picture
with your class.

Teacher: Children make a stick picture
and write a description.

CONNECTING
WRITING AND LANGUAGE

Read the sentences.
Which words tell how things look,
feel, sound, or taste?

Sam's gray cat is small . She is very quiet .
She drinks sweet milk. Sam pets her soft fur.

The blue words tell how things look, feel,
sound, and taste.
They are describing words.
You will learn about describing words.

Name _____

1 Describing How Things Taste and Smell

◆ Some **describing words** tell how things taste or smell.

taste

sweet   salty

sour

smell

smoky   fresh

An apple tastes sweet.
Sweet is a describing word.

A campfire smells smoky.
Smoky is a describing word.

▶ Tell how each thing tastes or smells.
Write a describing word for each picture.

1. _sour_

2. _____

3. _____

4. _____

Teacher: Children identify and write describing words.

Name ____________________

THINK AND REMEMBER

- Use **describing words** to tell how things taste or smell.

Practice

Read each sentence.
Write the describing word.

5. I like sour lemons. sour

6. I smell the fresh bread. ________

7. Do you like sweet apples? ________

8. We ate salty ham. ________

9. Dad made a smoky fire. ________

10. Let's eat some sweet raisins. ________

Application: See the ***Teacher's Edition.***

Name _____

2 Describing How Things Feel and Sound

◆ Some **describing words** tell how things feel or sound.

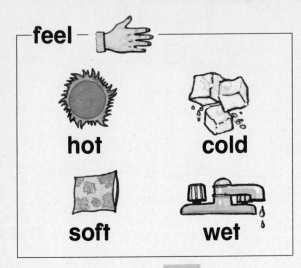

feel

hot   cold

soft   wet

sound

loud   quiet

The sun feels hot.   This lion sounds loud.
Hot is a describing word.   Loud is a describing word.

▶ Draw a line under the describing words that tell how things feel or sound.

1.   2.    3.    4.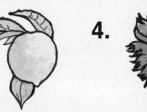

hot   cold   sour   loud

Write the describing words you drew a line under.

5.    6. _____   7. _____

Teacher: Children identify and write describing words.

THINK AND REMEMBER

◆ Use **describing words** to tell how things feel or sound.

Practice

■ Finish each sentence.
Write a describing word.

8. The lion has a ___ roar.

9. A ___ mouse hides.

10. I like the kitten's ___ fur.

11. Rain falls on the ___ grass.

12. The ___ snow falls.

13. Try this ___ soup.

3 Describing Words for Shapes and Sizes

◆ Some **describing words** tell about shape or size.

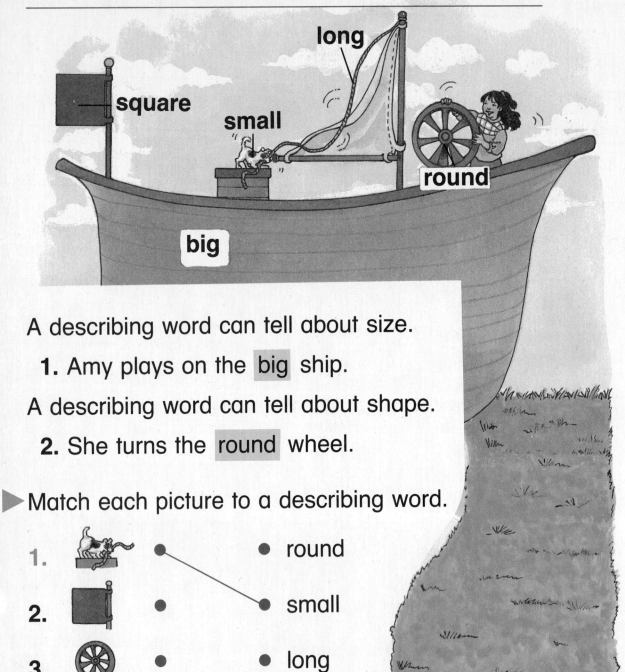

long

square

small

round

big

A describing word can tell about size.

1. Amy plays on the big ship.

A describing word can tell about shape.

2. She turns the round wheel.

▶ Match each picture to a describing word.

1. ● ● round

2. ● ● small

3. ● ● long

4. ● ● square

Teacher: Children identify and write describing words.

> **THINK AND REMEMBER**
> ◆ Use **describing words** to tell about shape or size.

Practice

■ Finish each sentence with a describing word.
The picture will help you.

5. Patch is a _____ small _____ dog.

6. He stands on the _____ box.

7. He has a _____ patch on one eye.

8. Patch pulls the _____ rope.

9. Up goes the sail on the _____ ship.

4 Describing Words for Colors

◆ Some **describing words** name colors.

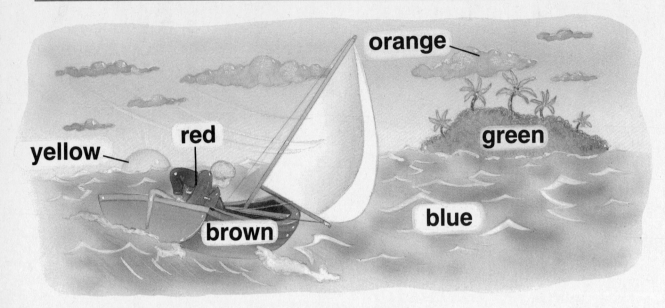

The words <u>yellow</u>, <u>red</u>, <u>orange</u>, <u>green</u>, <u>blue</u>, and <u>brown</u> name colors.

They are describing words.

Jason sails the blue sea.

▶ Write each describing word that names a color.

1. The yellow sun is bright.

2. Look at the orange clouds!

3. His brown boat is fast.

Teacher: Children identify and write describing words.

Name _____

THINK AND REMEMBER
◆ Use **describing words** to tell about color.

yellow

red

purple

Practice

■ Finish each sentence.
Write a describing word for color.

4. Jason found a ____ island.

green

5. Where is the ____ flag?

6. These ____ stones are pretty.

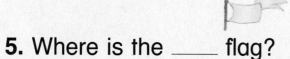

7. I'll put some in my ____ bag.

8. He sailed on the ____ sea.

Name _____

◆ Some **describing words** tell how many.

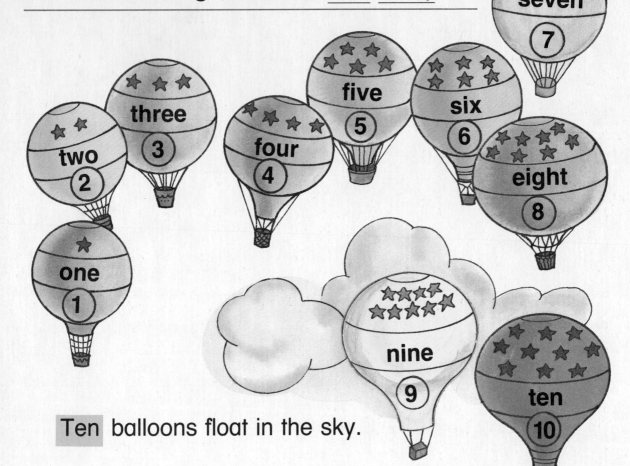

Ten balloons float in the sky.

▶ Match each picture to a word.

1. three •

2. six •   •

3. seven •

  •

4. four •   •

Teacher: Children identify and write describing words.

THINK AND REMEMBER

◆ Use describing words to tell <u>how</u> <u>many</u>.

Practice

■Finish each sentence.
Write the describing word that tells <u>how</u> <u>many</u>.

10

5. Do you see ___ten___ balloons?

1

6. _____ balloon is mine.

2

7. _____ balloons fly over a tree.

8

8. The other _____ balloons float higher.

5

9. These _____ balloons race.

Name _____

◆ Some **describing words** tell about the weather.

snowy

windy

sunny

rainy

▶ Match each picture to a describing word for weather.

1. ●   ● cloudy

2. ●   ● sunny

3. ●   ● snowy

4. ●   ● rainy

Teacher: Children identify and write describing words.

Name _____

THINK AND REMEMBER

◆ Use **describing words** to tell about weather.

Practice

■ Write a describing word for each sentence. Use a word from the box.

> sunny rainy cloudy windy

5. I go to the ___sunny___ beach.

6. Today it is _____ .

7. My kite flies on _____ days.

8. Do you like _____ days?

Describing Words with er and est

- Some **describing words** tell how two things are different.
- Some **describing words** tell how more than two things are different.

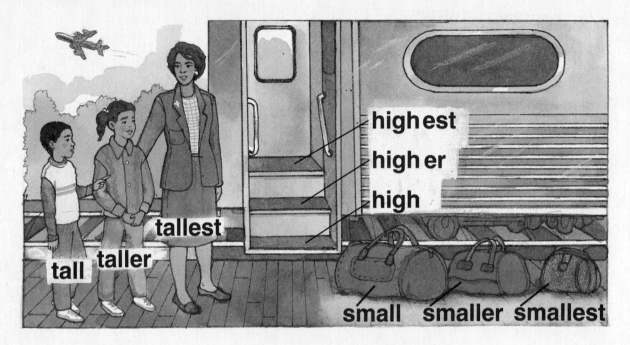

Add er to tell how two things are different.
Add est to tell how more than two things
are different.

▶ Read each sentence.
Draw a line under the correct describing word.

1. That is a (small, smallest) bag.

2. It is (smallest, smaller) than the blue one.

3. The red bag is the (smallest, small) of all.

Teacher: Children identify and write describing words.

Name _____

> ## THINK AND REMEMBER
> ◆ Use **describing words** with <u>er</u> and <u>est</u> to tell how things are different.

Practice

■ Finish each sentence.
Write the correct describing word.

(tall, tallest)

4. Brian is _____ tall _____ .

(taller, tallest)

5. His sister is _____ than he is.

(taller, tallest)

6. Mother is the _____ .

(faster, fastest)

7. This train is _____ than a car.

(faster, fastest)

8. The plane is the _____ of them all.

Building Vocabulary
Words That Mean Almost the Same Thing

Some words have almost the same meaning.

1. The children are quick.

2. The children are fast.

Practice

■ Read the word next to each picture.

Write a word from the box that has almost the same meaning.

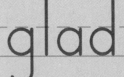

glad   upset
noisy   little

1. **happy** _____ glad _____

2. **loud** _____

3. **small** _____

4. **sad** _____

Teacher: Children write synonyms.

HBJ material copyrighted under notice appearing earlier in this work.

Name _____

Listening and Speaking

Listen to this poem.
Then read aloud the poem with your class.

The Little Hill
by Harry Behn

Windy shadows race
Over a hilly place
I know, a sunny place,
   A secret place.

It's not so far away,
I go there every day,
Every bright windy day
   I go there to play.

Teacher: Read aloud the poem. Children participate in a
choral reading.

Language Enrichment
Describing Words

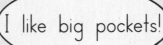

I like big pockets!

Finishing a Rhyme

Think about pockets, teddy bears, and rockets. Write describing words for the rhyme. Share your rhyme with your classmates.

_____

I like _____ pockets,

_____

_____ teddy bears, and

_____

_____ rockets!

Teacher: Children use describing words to complete the rhyme.

Name _____

CONNECTING
LANGUAGE AND WRITING

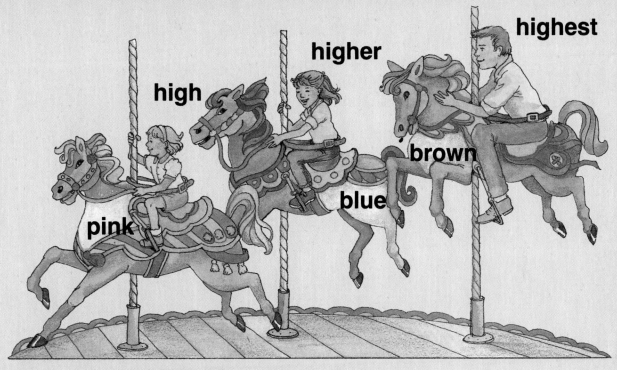

highest

higher

high

brown

blue

pink

Write about the picture.
Use describing words.

_____

- -

_____

- -

_____

- -

_____

- -

_____

Teacher: Children write sentences
about the picture.

Name _____

5 Unit Checkup

Description   pages 183–184

Kim's class wrote about a class trip.
Read the description and follow the directions.

The Forest

We walked through a quiet forest. The air smelled fresh. We saw small animals. One of them was eating.

1. Draw a line under the answer to the question. What do the sentences describe?

   a. a game   **b.** a forest

2. Draw a line around the words that tell about the forest.

   quiet   red   sad   fresh

Writing Process   pages 186–191

Kim's class changed a word in their description.
Draw a line around the new word.

3.

   We saw small ʌ animals.
              raccoons

Teacher: Read aloud the directions for each exercise.

Describing How Things Taste, Smell, Feel, and Sound   pages 194–197

Write a describing word from the box to tell about each picture.

smoky	sour
cold	loud

4. 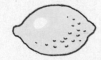 It tastes _____

5.  They feel _____

6. It sounds _____

7.  It smells _____

Describing Words for Shapes and Sizes   pages 198–199

Match each picture to a describing word.

8. •   • tall

9. •   • round

10. •   • small

Name _____

Describing Words for Colors and Numbers   pages 200–203

Draw a line under the describing words for color.
Write the words that tell <u>how many</u>.

_____

- - - - - - - -

11. Four girls ride in a blue car.   _____

_____

- - - - - - - -

12. Here are the two yellow boats.   _____

Describing Words for Weather   pages 204–205

Draw a line around the correct describing word
for each picture.

13.   sunny

cloudy

14.   windy

rainy

Describing Words with <u>er</u> and <u>est</u>   pages 206–207

Draw a line under the correct describing word.

15. The red string is (long, longest).

16. The blue string is even (longer, longest).

17. The green string is the (longer, longest) of all.

Telling Stories

◆ **COMPOSITION FOCUS: Story**
◆ **LANGUAGE FOCUS: Capital Letters and End Marks**

The Singing Monster

Name _____

Reading with a Writer's Eye

Listen to the story.
Tell the story.

 *from* Imogene's Antlers
by David Small

_____

- -

_____

- -

_____

- -

_____

Teacher: Read aloud the story in the *Teacher's Edition.* Children dictate or write sentences to retell it.

_____
- -
_____
_____
- -
_____
- -
_____
_____
- -
_____

Name _____

Thinking As a Writer
Studying a Story

Listen to part of <u>Imogene's Antlers.</u>
Who is the story about?
Where does the story take place?

> On Thursday, when Imogene woke up,
> she found she had grown antlers.
> Getting dressed was difficult, and going
> through a door now took some thinking.
> Imogene started down for breakfast.
> "OH!!" Imogene's mother fainted away.

What happens to Imogene in the story?

Teacher: Children discuss the character, setting,
and plot of the story.

READING ↔ WRITING CONNECTION   **219**

HBJ material copyrighted under notice appearing earlier in this work.

Thinking As a Writer
Telling What Happens Next

In the story Imogene's Antlers,
Imogene wakes up with antlers.
What do you think Imogene will do
at the end of the story?
Draw a picture.

Tell about your picture.

Teacher: Children predict what might
happen next in the story.

Listening and Speaking
Talking with Expression

These children are reading aloud <u>Imogene's Antlers</u>.
They are acting out the words as they read.

Choose a favorite story with your classmates.
Read aloud the story.
Act out the story as you read.

Getting Story Ideas

Roy wanted to write a story for his family.
He drew pictures of his ideas.
Then he chose his picture of a dragon named Pink Nano.
Talk about Roy's picture.

Try Your Hand

Think about stories you would like to tell.
Draw pictures of your ideas.
Choose one to write about.

WRITING PROCESS

Teacher: Children choose a story idea.

Planning Your Story

Roy thought about his story idea.
He drew pictures to show what happens.
Then he wrote sentences.

Pink Nano wanted to go to school.

Pink Nano came to school.

What happens to the character in Roy's story?

Try Your Hand

Draw pictures about your story idea.
Show what happens in the story.
Write a sentence about each picture.

2 Writing Your Story

Roy looked at his pictures and his sentences.
He wrote his story.

Pink Nano

Pink Nano is a dragon.
Once Pink Nano cried.
She wanted to come to
school. I asked my
teacher. Now Pink Nano
reads stories to us.
Pink Nano is smart!

Try Your Hand

What happens in your story?
Write a story to share with
someone at home.

Who? Why?
What?

WRITING PROCESS

Teacher: Children use their pictures and sentences to
write a story.

Teacher: Children write the first draft of their stories.　　COMPOSITION: DRAFTING　**225**

Name _____

WRITING PROCESS

3 Adding Story Details

Roy read his story to Carla.
They talked about what he
could add.
Roy added to his story.

Pink Nano

Pink Nano is a dragon.
Once Pink Nano cried.
She wanted to come to
school. I asked my
She said yes.
teacher. Now Pink Nano
reads stories to us.
Pink Nano is smart!

Use this mark ∧ .
Add to your story.

stories
She reads.
∧
She reads stories.

Try Your Hand

Read your story to a classmate.
What can you add?

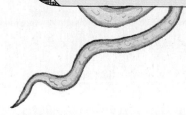

WRITING PROCESS

Teacher: Children discuss their stories and
revise them.

4 Checking Capital Letters and End Marks

Roy read his sentences.
He checked the capital letters and the end marks.
Find the capital letters and the end marks.

Pink Nano

Pink Nano is a dragon.
Once Pink Nano cried.
She wanted to come to
school. I asked my
teacher. ∧ Now Pink Nano
    She said yes.
reads stories to us.
Pink Nano is smart!

Try Your Hand

Read your story.
Make sure each sentence begins
with a capital letter.
Make sure each sentence has an
end mark.

Use this mark ≡.
Show where a
capital letter goes.

i̲ asked her.

I asked her.

WRITING PROCESS

Teacher: Children check capital letters and
punctuation in their stories.

5 | Sharing Your Story

Roy copied his story.
He made it into a card.
Then he gave it to his family.

> ## Pink Nano
>
> Pink Nano is a dragon.
> Once Pink Nano cried.
> She wanted to come to
> school. I asked my teacher.
> She said yes. Now Pink
> Nano reads stories to us.
> Pink Nano is smart!

Try Your Hand

Copy your story.
Share your story with someone at home.

WRITING PROCESS

Writing in the Content Areas
Physical Education

Play this game with a partner.
Think of your favorite animal.
Pretend you are the animal.
Finish the sentences.

I am a _____
_____
_____.

I can _____
_____
_____.

Now move like the animal.
Ask your partner to guess what kind of animal you are
pretending to be.
Then read aloud your sentences.

Teacher: Children write sentences and play a game.

Name _____

CONNECTING
WRITING AND LANGUAGE

Look for the capital letters and the end marks in this story.

One day a spaceman landed near our house . His name was Yomo .
Mom let him stay with us !
I like Yomo.

The blue letters are capital letters.
The yellow marks are end marks.
You will learn more about capital letters and end marks.

Teacher: Children identify capital letters and punctuation in the story.

CONNECTING WRITING AND LANGUAGE **231**

HBJ material copyrighted under notice appearing earlier in this work.

Name _____

◆ A sentence always begins with a **capital letter.**
◆ The word <u>I</u> is always written as a **capital letter.**

S ometimes **I** pretend.   **T** his game is fun.

▶ Draw a line around the letters that should be capital letters.

1. [m]y bunny can hop.   **2.** now i am a bunny.

Write each sentence correctly.

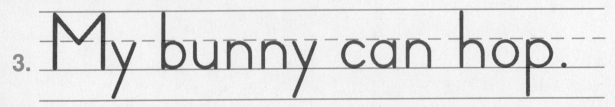

3. My bunny can hop.

4. _____

Teacher: Children identify and write letters that should be capital letters.

Name _____

THINK AND REMEMBER

◆ Begin a sentence with a **capital letter**.
◆ Write the word I as a **capital letter**.

Practice

■ Choose the correct word.
Write each sentence.

(i, I) watch the bird fly.

5.
I watch the bird fly.

(Then, then) I flap my arms.

6. _____

(The, the) bird sings well.

7. _____

So can (i, I)!

8. _____

HBJ material copyrighted under notice appearing earlier in this work.

2 Special Names

◆ The special name of a person, a place, or an animal begins with a **capital letter.**

Greg and Pep
live in Westwood.

Robin and King
live in Dodson.

▶ Write the special names.

King

1. King   dog

2. city   Westwood

3. Robin   girl

Teacher: Children identify and write names.

THINK AND REMEMBER

◆ Begin the special name of a person, a place, or an animal with a **capital letter.**

Practice

■ Write a special name in each sentence. The pictures will help you.

a boy

4. Greg writes me a letter.

a turtle

5. _____ sleeps in the sun.

a girl

6. I miss my friend _____.

a city

7. It snows in _____.

a dog

8. _____ has warm fur.

Titles of Books

◆ Each important word in a book title begins with a **capital letter.**

Alicia reads A Pocket for Corduroy.

▶ Draw a line around the capital letters in each book title.

1. The Man in the Moon

2. The Tiny Dinosaur

3. Dozens of Dolls

4. Jolly Otter

Teacher: Children identify and write important words in titles of books.

THINK AND REMEMBER

◆ Begin each important word in a book title with a **capital letter**.

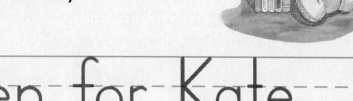

Practice

■ Write the book titles correctly.

a kitten for kate

5. A Kitten for Kate

my magic kite

6. _____

a circus in town

7. _____

one cold winter

8. _____

brian and friends

9. _____

4 End Marks

◆ A telling sentence ends with a **.**.
◆ An asking sentence ends with a **?**.
◆ A sentence that shows strong feeling ends with an **!**.

**Look at this great book!
Let's read it.**

**What is
it called?**

▶ Read each sentence.
Draw a line around the correct end mark.

1. This book is new   **.**   **?**   **!**

2. Who gave the book to you   **.**   **?**   **!**

3. Mrs. Hall gave it to me   **.**   **?**   **!**

4. Look at the pretty pictures   **.**   **?**   **!**

Teacher: Children identify and write end marks.

Name  _____

Practice

■ Write each sentence with the correct end mark.

This is a castle

5.  This is a castle.

It looks huge

6. _____

Who lives in it

7. _____

A king lives there

8. _____

Do you know the king

9. _____

Building Vocabulary
Sound Words

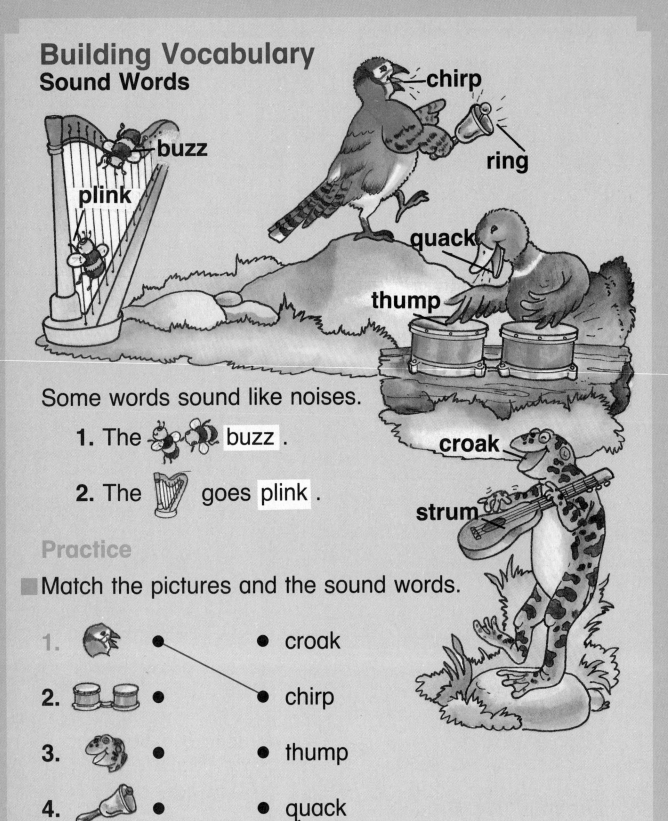

Some words sound like noises.

1. The 🐝🐝 buzz .

2. The 🎵 goes plink .

Practice

▦ Match the pictures and the sound words.

1. 🐦 •   • croak

2. 🥁 •   • chirp

3. 🐸 •   • thump

4. 🔔 •   • quack

5. 🦆 •   • ring

Teacher: Children match pictures to sound words.

Name _____

Poetry

Listen to this poem.
Then read aloud the poem with your class.

The Harbor
by Olive Beaupré Miller

Look, see the boat!
Where? On the sea!
Swish through the waves it goes
Swish through the sea!

Look, see the smoke;
See its funnels red!
Hark, hear the whistle!
Woo-oo-oo! the whistle said.

Teacher: Read aloud the poem. Children
participate in a choral reading.

Name _____

Language Enrichment
Capital Letters and End Marks

Darcy the Dog

On Saturday I went for a walk. Can you guess what I saw? It was a talking dog. What a surprise that was!

Make-believe Storybook

1. Write a make-believe story about a person, a place, or an animal.
2. Use some asking sentences.
   Make some sentences show strong feeling.
3. Draw pictures for your story.
4. Write a title for your story.
5. Make a storybook.

Teacher: Children write, illustrate, and share stories.

Name _____

CONNECTING
LANGUAGE AND WRITING

What do you see through the make-believe window?
Draw a picture.

My Make-believe Window

Write a sentence about what you see.

_____

- -

_____

- -

_____

Teacher: Children draw pictures and
write sentences about them.

6 Unit Checkup

Story   pages 219–220

Max wrote this story.
Read the story and follow the directions.

> ## The Silly Hat
>
> Jeff made a paper hat. He put it on.
> The hat made him laugh. Jeff wears
> the hat when he plays.

1. Draw a line under the answer to the question.
Which sentence tells about the story?

    a. Jeff loses a hat.   **b.** Jeff has a silly hat.

2. What do you think Jeff will do next?
Draw a line around the picture.

Teacher: Read aloud the directions for each exercise.

Writing Process   pages 222–229

Draw a line around the part Max added to his story.
Draw a line under the capital letter and the end mark.

3.

silly

Jeff wears the ^hat when he plays.

Using Capital Letters   pages 232–233

Write each sentence correctly.

mom and i pretend.

4. _____

we act like monkeys.

5. _____

Special Names   pages 234–235

Draw a line around each special name.

6. I live in Hillside.

7. Mittens is my cat.

8. Where is Alex?

9. He lives on Oak Lane.

Titles of Books   pages 236–237

Write the book titles correctly.

rainy day games

- -

10. _____

bears in a bus

- -

11. _____

a trip to mars

- -

12. _____

the talking dog

- -

13. _____

End Marks   pages 238–239

Draw a line around the correct end mark
for each sentence.

14. This is a special window   .   ?   !

15. What do you see   .   ?   !

16. I see a star   .   ?   !

17. It's a shooting star   .   ?   !

WORD BANK

Name _____

Naming Words

Animals		People	
	bird		baby
	cat		boy
	dinosaur		brother
	dog		girl
	fish		father
	mouse		mother
	rabbit		sister

More Animals

_____

- - - - - - - - - - - - - -

_____

_____

More People

_____

- - - - - - - - - - - - - -

_____

_____

Teacher: Children may use the **Word Bank** as a reference.

Name _____

Naming Words

Places

 city

 farm

 house

 library

 park

 school

 store

Things

 apple

 bicycle

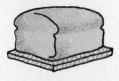 bread

 car

 pencil

 shoe

 truck

WORD BANK

More Places

_____

- - - - - - - - - - - - -

_____

_____

- - - - - - - - - - - - -

More Things

_____

- - - - - - - - - - - - -

_____

_____

- - - - - - - - - - - - -

HBJ material copyrighted under notice appearing earlier in this work.

Name _____

Special Naming Words

Months of the Year

1. January   2. February   3. March
4. April   5. May   6. June
7. July   8. August   9. September
10. October   11. November   12. December

Days of the Week

1. Sunday   2. Monday   3. Tuesday
4. Wednesday   5. Thursday   6. Friday
7. Saturday

Holidays

 Mother's Day   Fourth of July

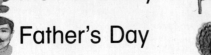 Father's Day   Thanksgiving

More Holidays

Teacher: Children may use the **Word Bank** as a reference.

Action Words

 climb

 run

 cook

 sing

 cry

 swim

 fly

 talk

 kick

 wave

 pull

More Action Words

_____

_____

_____

_____

 push

Describing Words

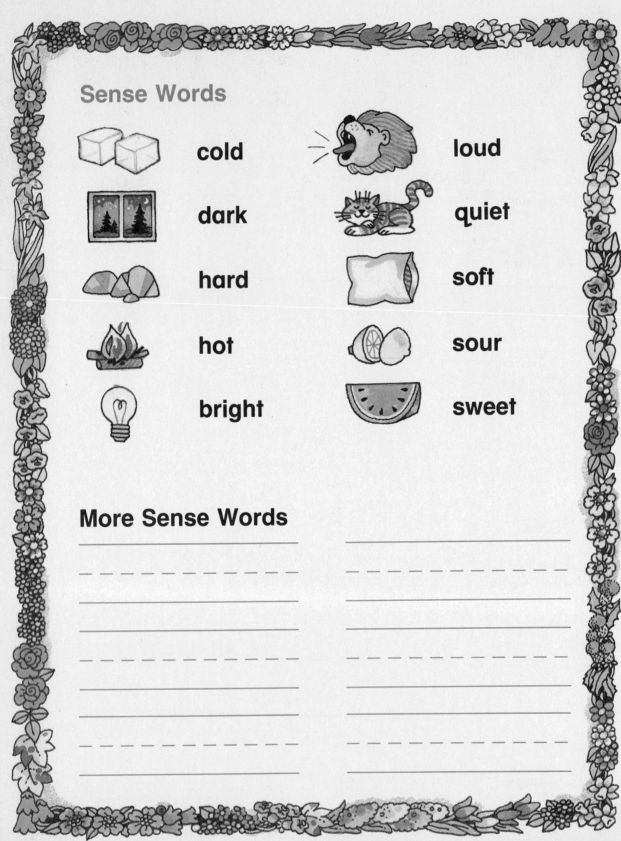

Sense Words

cold

dark

hard

hot

bright

loud

quiet

soft

sour

sweet

More Sense Words

_____   _____

_____   _____

_____   _____

_____   _____

_____   _____

_____   _____

Teacher: Children may use the **Word Bank** as a reference.

Name _____

Shapes

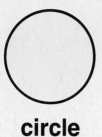  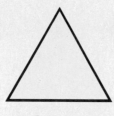 

circle   square   triangle   rectangle

More Shapes

_____   _____

- - - - - - - - - - - - - - -   - - - - - - - - - - - - - - -

_____   _____

Color Words

 blue   orange

 brown   red

 green   yellow

More Colors

_____   _____

- - - - - - - - - - - - - - -   - - - - - - - - - - - - - - -

_____   _____

WORD BANK

Teacher: Children may use the **Word Bank** as a reference.

Describing Words

Weather Words

 cloudy

 snowy

 rainy

 sunny

More Weather Words

_____   _____

- - - - - - - - - - - - - - - - -   - - - - - - - - - - - - - - - - -

Feeling Words

 angry

 sad

 excited

 scared

 happy

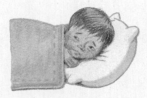 sick

More Feeling Words

_____   _____

- - - - - - - - - - - - - - - - -   - - - - - - - - - - - - - - - - -

Teacher: Children may use the **Word Bank** as a reference.

Name _____

Rhyming Words

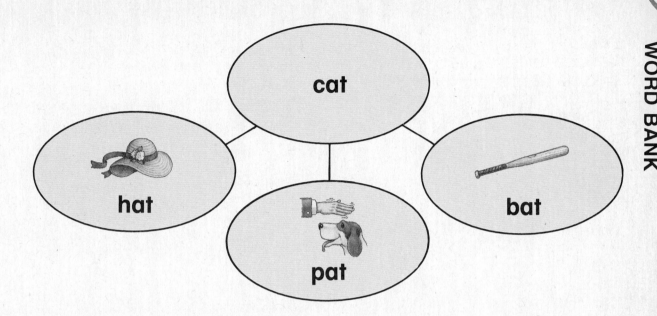

More Rhyming Words

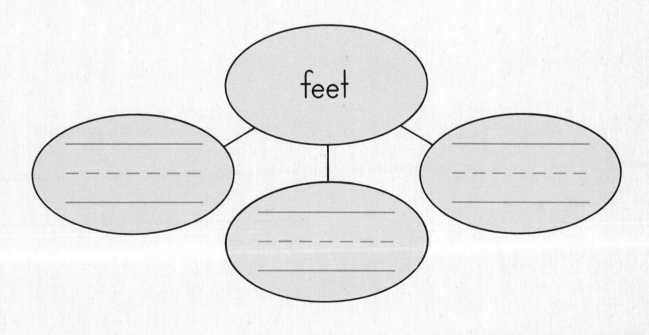

Teacher: Children may use clusters to generate rhyming words.

Name _____

Rhyming Words

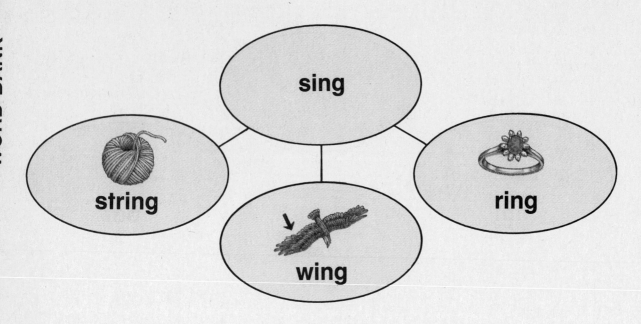

More Rhyming Words

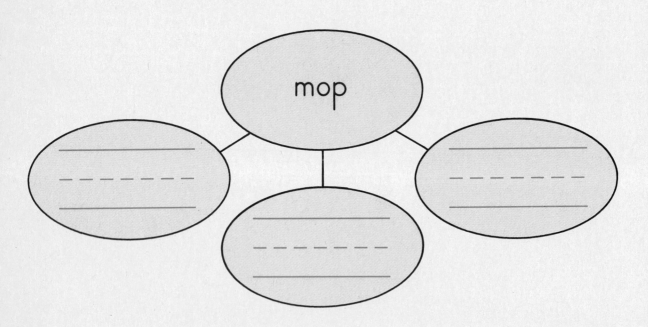

Teacher: Children may use clusters to generate rhyming words.

HBJ material copyrighted under notice appearing earlier in this work.

Names in boldface refer to the punchouts at the back of the Pupil Book.

N 8
O 9
P 0
Q 1
R 2

A Look at Me

by

P2

P4

Puppets

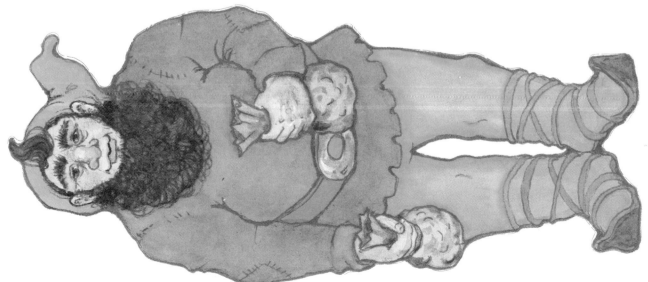

Teacher: Children punch out puppets, glue them on craft sticks, and use them to retell *Jack and the Beanstalk*.

P6

Sentences

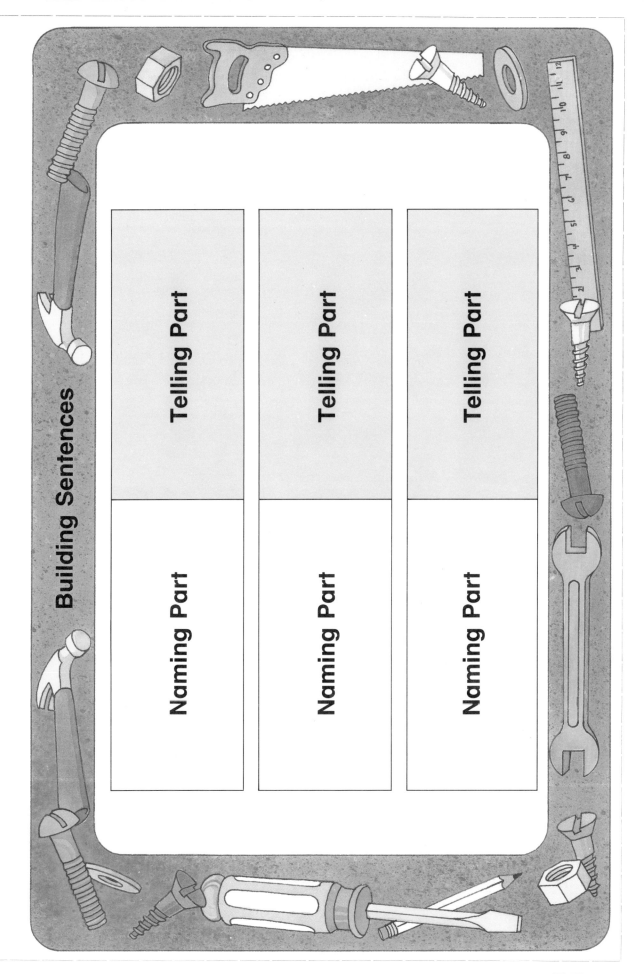

Building Sentences

Naming Part	Telling Part
Naming Part	Telling Part
Naming Part	Telling Part

Teacher: Children use naming parts and telling parts to build and share their sentences. Further instructions are in the *Teacher's Edition.*

P8

Sentences

My robot	is new.
This toy	walks and talks.
It	sings songs.
The children	go to the zoo.
Lisa and Kim	watch the monkeys.
The monkeys	swing from the trees.

Teacher: Children use the yellow and blue cards to build their own sentences. Further instructions are in the *Teacher's Edition.*

P10 **Teacher:** Children write their own sentence parts.

Revising Visor

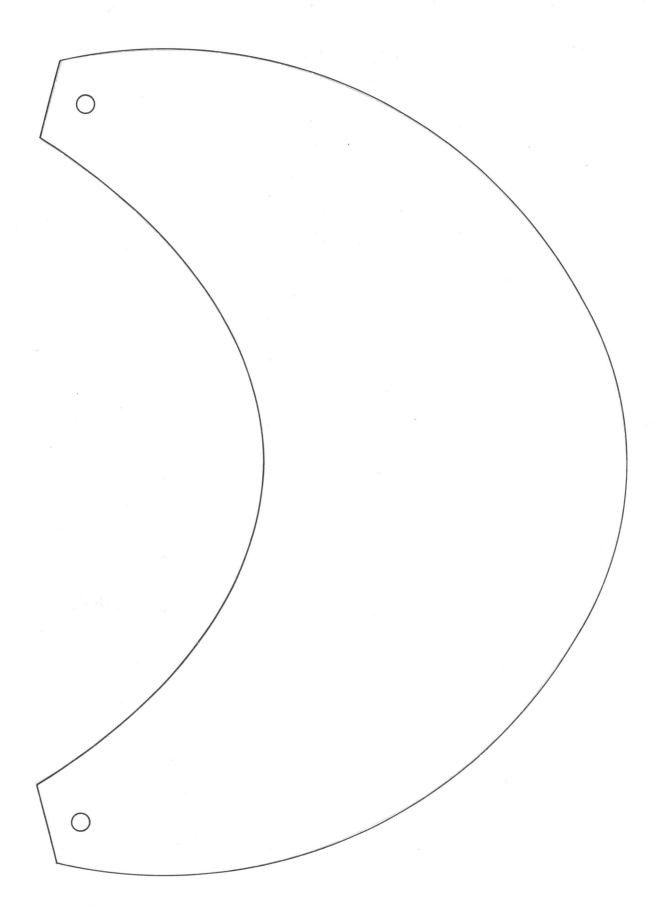

Teacher: Children punch out visor, decorate it, and add string.
Children wear visors when they revise their writing.

P12

Naming Word Village

Teacher: Further instructions are in the *Teacher's Edition.*

Naming Word Village

P16

Naming Words and Action Words Game

My friends | Two bugs | Those girls | Three ducks

My friend | One bug | The girl | The duck

Those mothers | The clowns | These boys | The monkeys

My mother | The clown | A boy | This monkey

Teacher: Children play a subject-verb agreement game. See the *Teacher's Edition* for directions.

P18

Naming Words and Action Words Game

laughs.	plays.	eats.	grows.
laugh.	play.	eat.	grow.
works.	turns.	sings.	runs.
work.	turn.	sing.	run.

P20

Opposite and Alike Games

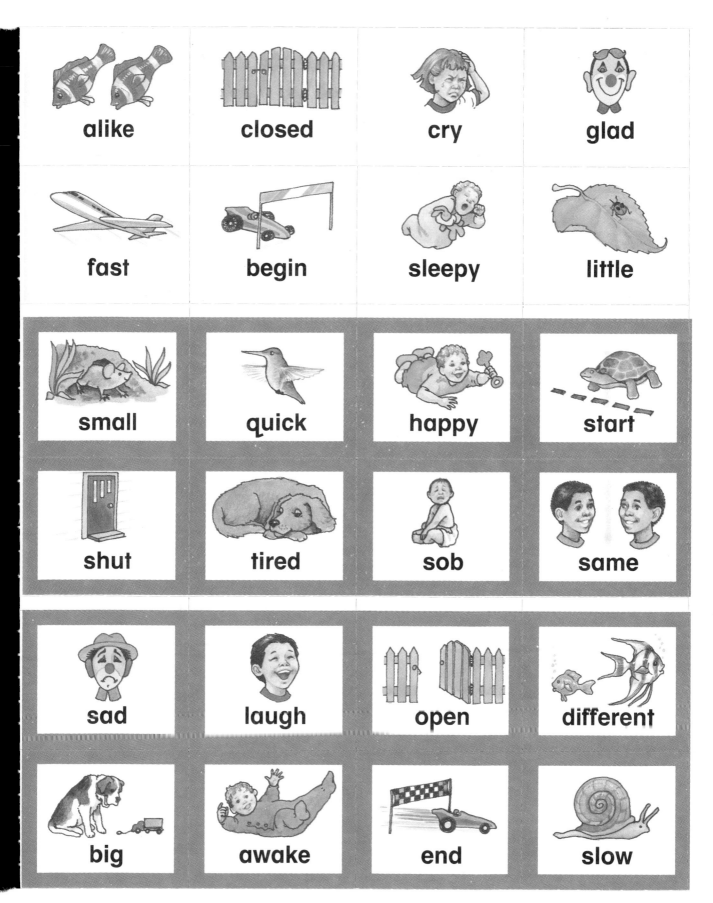

alike	closed	cry	glad
fast	begin	sleepy	little
small	quick	happy	start
shut	tired	sob	same
sad	laugh	open	different
big	awake	end	slow

Teacher: Children use yellow and orange cards for a synonym game and orange and purple cards for an antonym game.

P22

The Story Game

Teacher: Children use the game to tell a story. See the *Teacher's Edition* for directions.

P24

The Story Game

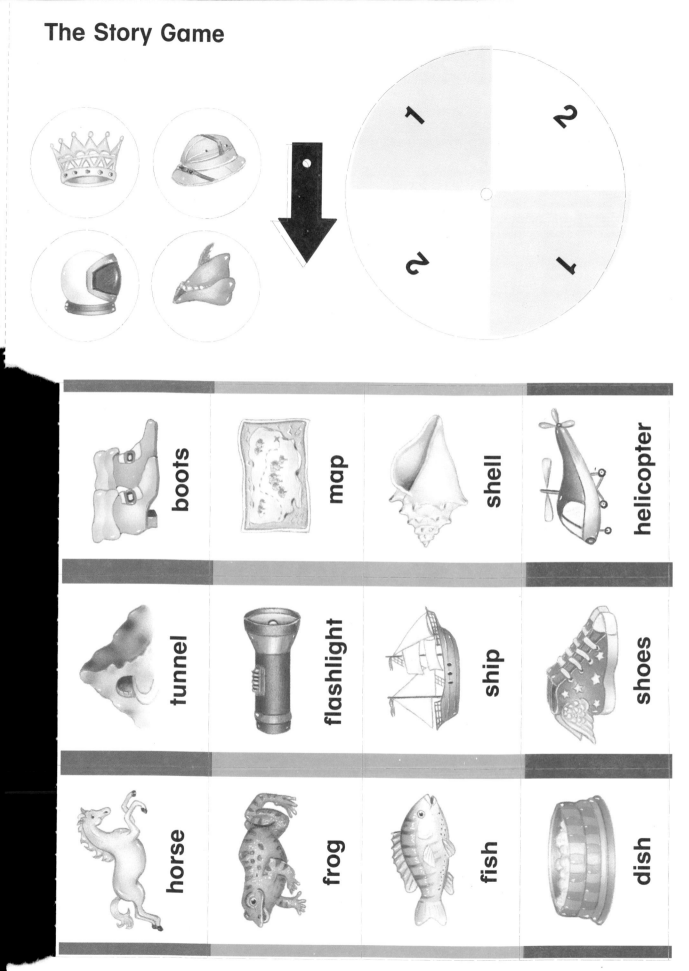

boots

map

shell

helicopter

tunnel

flashlight

ship

shoes

horse

frog

fish

dish

P26